W9-DCH-240

341.3
P
c.1

PINTO
SPY CATCHER

Spy-catcher

Spy-catcher

BY ORESTE PINTO

HARPER & BROTHERS, NEW YORK

341.3
P
c. 1

Library of Congress catalog card number: 52-12125

Contents

v

Spy-catcher

CHAPTER I

Introduction

My main job in life has been to catch spies. During the last war I was personally responsible for the execution of seven spies and for long terms of imprisonment for a great many more. I do not quote these facts out of vanity but rather as my credentials for writing a book on spies. Whatever the following pages may lack in literary merit, the information they contain is at least authentic.

During a series of lectures I have given since returning from active Counter-Intelligence work, many people, young and old, men and women, have asked me how they could become official C.I. agents. Most of them, impressed by the countless films, novels and supposedly authentic books on spies, were attracted by the idea of an exciting career in which glamorous spies were tracked down in the bars of luxury hotels, in which there were secret signs and passwords, thrilling pursuits in fast cars and "getting your man" after an arduous chase which might culminate in cornering the quarry in the sewers of Vienna, or some other exotic foreign capital. There is indeed excitement at times in the life of a real spy-catcher and occasionally some risks and, rarely, the danger of losing one's life. But just as service on the battlefield is a long stretch of tedious wait-

1

ing, punctuated by small flashes of danger, so also is the career of a real-life spy-catcher. The films or the novel set out to entertain their public. They have to concentrate on the high lights of the plot and skip over the long grueling hours of routine investigations, of monotonous inquiry and the slow piecing together of the jigsaw of clues.

The potential spy-catcher needs at least ten qualities, seven of which he must be born with and only three of which can be acquired by his own efforts. Right from the start, therefore, most potential Counter-Intelligence agents are handicapped in their quest. In the following paragraphs I will enumerate these necessary qualities, roughly in their order of importance as I see it.

The first is a *phenomenal memory*. This is doubly essential. The spy-catcher must not only be able to memorize faces, events and places, which he may come across many years later, but he should also be able to conduct an interrogation, lasting several days perhaps, without having to take notes. Later I shall write in more detail about interrogations but, briefly, one of the prime factors is to get the confidence of the suspect and, if possible, to lull him into a sense of false confidence. If the investigator has to keep on breaking off his questions to take down notes, he loses all opportunity of turning the formal occasion into what is seemingly an informal chat and the suspect remains on his guard. Worse still, the suspect is given time between questions, while the interrogator is busy scribbling away, to regroup his thoughts and consider suitable replies against further questions. The investigator who can sit back apparently at ease may give the suspect the feeling that this is merely official routine and may thus trap him into over-confidence ending in self-betrayal.

I myself have been blessed—or cursed—with an exceptional memory. I can, for example, remember exactly not only what presents were given to me on my third birthday but who gave them and at what time of the day they arrived. My very earliest memories go back to the age of six months and I can still recall accurate impressions of my cot and the frilly flounces that hung around it. My father had one of the first telephones to be installed in Holland. Important local numbers were written on a sheet of paper that hung beside the instrument. This was over fifty years ago and I can still remember each of those telephone numbers exactly. I am not stating these facts out of boastfulness. It is through no virtue or hard endeavor on my part that my memory should have been exceptional. But without such a memory I should never have made a catcher of spies.

Next comes a double quality—*great patience and regard for detail*. A good example of this is given in Chapter VII of this book, dealing with the strange case of the patriotic Mynheer Dronkers. There is no need, therefore, for me to dwell here on the usefulness of patience and regard for detail to the Counter-Intelligence officer, except to say that when a spy is fighting for his life in an interrogation he will obviously exercise all the patience he can muster. His life depends on it. His interrogator must be able to show greater patience if he is to succeed. Again, an efficient spy, and inefficient spies do not last long, will obviously have

3

the main outlines of his story committed to memory. It is most unlikely that any interrogator could trip him up on the important aspects of his story, many of which in any case will be based on fact and the others as near to actuality as possible. It is only in the minor details that the clever spy may go wrong or may have failed to provide himself with a plausible story. This eye for detail, coupled with apparently inexhaustible patience, thus becomes an important weapon in the hands of the interrogator.

Third on my list comes *a gift for languages*. However well a man can express himself in his own tongue, he is obviously restricted if he can question a suspect only through an interpreter. He will be unable to detect whether a detainee who claims to be a Swedish businessman, for example, is indeed so or is really a German or a Norwegian with an excellent knowledge of Swedish. When it comes to searching a suspect's belongings, the best detective in the world would be useless if he could not understand the language in which letters, diaries and official documents belonging to the suspect are written. Perhaps I may add here, again as fact and not as boasting, that I am lucky to have this knack for learning languages—having complete mastery of Dutch, Flemish, English, French, German and Italian, with a competent working knowledge of Spanish, Portuguese, Danish, Swedish, Norwegian, Rumanian and Swahili.

The fourth attribute of the Counter-Intelligence agent must be a *knowledge of practical psychology*. He must be able to assess shrewdly the character of the man he is inter-

4

rogating in order to know what line his questions should follow. Threats or a hectoring tone only act as a stiffener to the moral fiber of some suspects, yet a little sympathy, a few kind remarks, will help to break down their resistance. Others react in a totally opposite manner. Some spies are vain and can be made garrulous through judicious praise. And so on. The examiner who cannot from an early stage in the interrogation sum up his opponent's character is like a boxer going into the ring blindfolded.

The fifth attribute is *courage*. This may seem a strange remark and perhaps the reader will think that there is little courage required in acting as an examiner. Surely, you may say, it is the suspect fighting for his life who requires courage? That is true. No spy, however foolish his actions may be, lacks bravery, since he is prepared to risk his life in a foreign country on a lonely task which lacks the bolstering-up effect of comradeship in the ranks and which carries no recognition of his valor. It may, however, be evident from these few pages that the spy-catcher is the complete counterpart of the spy and must possess all the latter's own qualities, plus the essential wit or brains to defeat his opponent. Anyone who has listened to a Parliamentary debate or has attended an important trial where witnesses are cross-examined will know that there is a quality which I can only loosely call "moral superiority." That quality does not necessarily belong to the prosecutor but may be found on the side of the defense. It is a form of manifest courage, and in his way the Counter-Intelligence interrogator must try to establish it against the suspect. Not by ill-treating

5

him in any way but by believing more strongly in the rightness of his task than the suspect believes in his. If the interrogator can win this silent battle of wills he is a long way toward establishing his case. And for that he needs courage of a high moral order.

The sixth quality required in the spy-catcher is an almost *Baedeker-like knowledge of the capitals and important towns in Europe.* By this I mean that he must know not only the main streets and the important buildings but side streets, restaurants, hotels, local characteristics and distances from one point to another as well. All these facts must be stored in his mind in such a way that he can call on them at will. (Here, of course, we come back to the first attribute I mentioned—memory.) I can best illustrate my point by giving an example which occurred in an actual cross-examination.

It was March, 1942, when Hans was brought to my office for questioning. (He was subsequently acquitted through a technicality and I cannot, therefore, give his real name.) I leaned back in my chair as he sat down and studied him closely. He was tall and thin but strong and completely in control of himself. The cropped fair hair, steel-blue eyes, high cheekbones and sunken cheeks would have spelled out the word "German" even without the dueling scar that slashed his right cheek and which seemed to sign the testimony of his other features. Yet there were good Germans as well as bad ones, as I knew. The problem was—which was Hans?

His story was a simple, straightforward one. He had not

6

spoken many sentences before I realized that here was a man who was not only well educated, but highly intelligent and resolute into the bargain. He admitted frankly to being a German but claimed to have fled to Denmark in 1936 since his open opposition to the Nazis had endangered his life and property. In Copenhagen he had practiced as a solicitor and had built up a comfortable livelihood. But when the Nazis overran Denmark in 1940 he realized that he was in greater danger than before. So he had gone underground, had deliberately entered the lion's den by working his way back into Germany and thence across the border into Switzerland, from Switzerland to southern France and across the Spanish frontier to Barcelona. This was a genuine escape route, as I well knew.

I questioned him closely on the early part of his story. It was soon evident that he must have lived in Copenhagen for several years. He knew the city intimately. It also seemed likely that he had practiced as a solicitor from the legal phrases he used almost unconsciously. It seemed equally obvious that he had traveled the genuine escape route as he was able to tell me details which only a traveler along the route would remember. So far, so good.

I sat back and lit a cigarette. "Tell me," I asked in German, "what time in the day did you reach Barcelona?"

"It was late in the evening. About ten o'clock, perhaps."

"Where did you spend the night?"

"At the Hotel Continental."

"Ah yes, the Continental. Do you remember what floor the restaurant was on?" I asked.

7

There was the slightest pause and then he broke into a charming smile. "I'm afraid I don't know. You see, it was so late when I arrived—about ten o'clock, as I said. They told me the restaurant was closed so I had a light supper in my room."

"I see." It was a good answer and cleverly avoided my question. "And then next morning—what did you do?"

"I breakfasted in my room and then left the hotel. I went to the British Passport Office."

"How did you get there—by taxi or on foot?"

"I walked," he said.

"Wasn't that rather odd? You were a complete stranger in the town and yet you walked to a place you'd never been to before."

"I was afraid to travel by taxi. Spain is friendly with the Axis. The Gestapo has agents everywhere. I thought that taxi drivers might be in the pay of the Gestapo. And I look a typical German, don't I?" He grinned ruefully and touched his dueling scar with his finger tips.

I nodded. It was quite a reasonable excuse. "How then did you find your way?"

"I asked the policemen on duty."

"And how long did it take you to walk from the Hotel Continental to the British Passport Office?"

"About twenty minutes," he replied.

There was a pause. I took out a cigarette, tapped it on the case, lit it and inhaled deeply. "My friend," I said, "you are a liar. A clever liar but undoubtedly a liar—and probably a spy as well."

8

He went red and sprang up. "How dare you accuse me like that!" he shouted.

"Take it easy," I said. "Sit down. The act is over. There is no need to brazen it out."

I leaned forward. "Two points condemn you. Unlike almost every hotel in Europe the Continental has its restaurant not on the ground floor but on the second floor. You suspected a trap and cleverly skirted round it by saying the restaurant was closed when you arrived at ten that night. And so it would have been—in Berlin, or London, or Copenhagen. But what you didn't realize, my friend, is that in Spain, as in most countries bordering the Mediterranean, the night life begins much later than in Northern Europe. You have heard of taking a siesta—an afternoon nap? All hot countries indulge in the practice. The coolest part of the twenty-four hours, when people enjoy themselves, is late at night. Cinemas and theaters in Spain do not open until about eleven o'clock. So, you see, the restaurant in the Hotel Continental would not have been closed at ten. It would have been at its busiest, thronged with customers. The deduction is simple. You never went to the Continental."

He was about to blurt out something so I hurried on.

"There is no need to interrupt me. Even if that mistake did not convict you, this one would." I picked up a piece of paper and a pencil from my desk. "Watch. Since your knowledge of Barcelona is—shall I say, elementary?—I will draw you a little diagram. Here is the Hotel Continental—on the Rambla de Cataluña. Just further on is a large

9

square, the Plaza de Cataluña—see, I sketch it on the paper. Leading out of the square at the far end is the Paseo de Gracia. And just here, on the Paseo is the British Passport Office. It is not five minutes' walk from the Hotel Continental—you can't, as they say here in England, miss it. Yet you say you took twenty minutes to walk the distance. A tall, vigorous fellow like you could not be so slow a walker."

I rang the bell for the guards to take him away. "In fact," I added, "if you had really stayed at the Continental, which of course you did not, you would in all probability have been able to see the British Passport Office from your bedroom window. You certainly reached the Passport Office, the officials there confirm it. But I wonder how you arrived. In the back of a closed car belonging to the German Intelligence Service?"

As mentioned above, Hans did not pay the supreme penalty for being a spy but through a technicality was acquitted at the subsequent trial. Nevertheless I am convinced that he was a spy, and a dangerous one at that. He was interned for the rest of the war so that at least he could not actively follow his chosen career. The moral of this story is that cleverer men than I might have spent hours interrogating Hans but had they not possessed the Baedeker knowledge of foreign cities, in this case Barcelona, they would not have spotted the two tiny mistakes in his otherwise strong and credible account of himself.

The seventh attribute which the Counter-Intelligence officer must possess is *a thorough knowledge of interna-*

10

tional law. Every suspect, no matter what his nationality may be, has certain rights and privileges under international law. He cannot be detained for more than a certain length of time; certain conditions have to be observed during the course of his detention. Even if it were not anathema to the sense of British justice, international law would still prevent ill-treatment of prisoners and suspects. A clever spy, who is well versed in the details of the Hague Convention, might be able to thwart his interrogator by bluff, claiming protection under international law beyond his entitlement. The interrogator must, therefore, be able to match and outwit the suspect in this as in other aspects of their duel.

Next the spy-catcher must be *a born actor.* He must be able to simulate rage, or impatience, or sympathy, without at any time losing the rigid control of his emotions. I have already spoken of the practical psychology that comes into play when dealing with a suspect. This attribute is perhaps a counterpart of the other. Having assessed the suspect's personality and decided on the best method of tackling him, the interrogator must be able to act his part. It is no good adopting a hectoring tone when the eyes are still mild and the voice betrays sympathetic inflections. Conversely, the interrogator will soon give himself away if he adopts the tactics of sympathy and forgets to put off the acute glance and the edge to the voice. A good spy will himself be an adept at summing up his opponents. He will soon recognize the false note in the voice and the wintry smile which does not cloak the real purpose. Further, the spy-

11

catcher must be able to hide his real feelings as well as assume a false appearance. The suspect may have made a tiny slip and be unaware of it. The interrogator must pursue the point, but casually and without apparent interest. If a gleam in his eye or a tenseness in his manner betrays his inner excitement, the suspect will be on his guard, alert for further questions. Again, interrogations can become boring affairs when, for days on end, a stubborn suspect will continue to repeat the same story over and over again. The interrogator may in spite of himself become bored or seething with impatience. But he must rigidly suppress those feelings and never permit a gesture or a facial expression to betray his inner thoughts.

The ninth attribute is *the gift of detection*. In many ways this is a highly developed sense of logic. It is the ability to perceive cause and effect, to test mentally each link in the chain of evidence set before one by the suspect. Every efficient spy will have a plausible story—on the surface. Only the interrogator who can delve below the surface and bring to light by questioning any concealed evidence will succeed against the competent spy. Here the time factor is of great importance. A suspect should in theory be able to account for every minute of the time spent during the period under survey. On the other hand, an honest man, particularly under the stress of emotion, may not tell an entirely plausible story. He may at the first telling omit both details and major incidents through confusion or genuine forgetfulness. Few people indeed, as any police constable will testify, can give a coherent account of

12

some happening, starting at the beginning and covering every point to the end. Unless they are trained to give evidence, they will leave out important facts, blurt out what they recall in the wrong sequence and often repeat themselves. Two witnesses of a street accident may give quite different accounts of what they saw with their own eyes. The reader, appreciating this, can imagine how much more confused will be the story of a refugee, overwrought by relief at having reached safety and by the strain and privations he may have undergone en route. He may also have traveled by night across completely strange territory. There will be understandable gaps in his story and he may genuinely forget, if his travels have lasted days, weeks or even months, on what day and at what time of the day he crossed that frontier or reached this town. The Counter-Intelligence officer must have the ability to sift the true statement from the false, to make allowances for genuine loss of memory and for exaggeration caused through overstrain.

So far I have centered my remarks mainly on the verbal interrogation of suspects. In the following chapter I shall speak in more detail of the methods of interrogation, bringing in the searching of a suspect's property. I need only add here that all the belongings of a refugee are important in establishing or refuting his credentials, from the clothes he wears to the baggage he carries. Only a trained investigator, knowing what clues he is looking for, can possibly deduce the real evidence from searching letters, books, clothing and even parts of the body. The exceptional spy alone can

13

afford to trust his memory on codes or foreign addresses to which information is to be sent. The others will have notes or reminders hidden away. The investigator must not only know the different places where such incriminating evidence can be hidden but also approximately what kind of evidence he is searching for. I have already referred to the case of Mynheer Dronkers which is told in a later chapter. This strange case not only exemplifies the need for colossal patience but also shows the need of knowing what to look for.

Finally the tenth attribute of the spy-catcher must be *practical experience of previous "dodges."* There are certain well-known methods for secret writing or for concealing vital evidence. One of the great drawbacks of the German intelligence system in both world wars was their rigid following of routine and their apparent lack of initiative. Once a particular secret method or code had been broken, it should have been dropped at once and a substitute found. The Germans, however, often persevered with the same method long after it had been discovered and thus unnecessarily risked the lives of their spies. I should like to give two examples, one from the Second World War and one from the First.

In the First World War, when fighting took place on the Continent throughout, the spy's problem was not so much the acquiring of information but the passing of it. In the Second World War the problems tended to be reversed, largely through two inventions that had been made or perfected in the meantime—radio telegraphy and mi-

14

crophotography. A high-powered short-wave transmitter could easily be set up in a lonely part of, say, the Essex marshes, a message be transmitted and the set dismantled and driven miles away long before it could be monitored and the source of the message accurately located. Even more ingenious and elusive was the microcamera. I have seen a German model which was no longer than a fountain pen and roughly three times as thick. It could be clipped to an inside coat or waistcoat pocket. It could be used for filming a document, and the negative could be reduced to literally the size of a pinhead. A spy need only place the negative *under* the stamp on an envelope and send the letter to a foreign address. The actual letter would of course be quite harmless. The overloaded wartime Censors' Department would never have the time to steam off every stamp on business letters sent to a Lisbon address, say, in case there was a minute and easily overlooked negative stuck underneath. Unfortunately for themselves the German agents would continue to send letters to foreign addresses already under suspicion. Such letters were examined with even more than the normal care and before long this ingenious method was discovered.

My second example is taken from the First World War. This incident took place in 1916 on the French front near the Somme. It so happened that part of a village lay in No Man's Land and the rest of it behind the French lines. During a lull in the fighting the villagers, with the stolidity of country people, tried to pick up the threads of their rudely disturbed communal life. One peasant woman who lived

15

on the side of the village in German hands used to travel every day across the shell-shattered open space to visit her brother, whose cottage was behind the French lines. On reaching the French lines she was examined and questioned by a Counter-Intelligence officer every day as a routine check but, like all the other villagers who passed to and fro, she appeared to be quite harmless. One day on her return from her brother's cottage she arrived at the check post carrying a basket with her lunch in it. It was a homely meal of boiled eggs, bread and butter. The Counter-Intelligence officer had by now become used to her and greeted her in a friendly tone. He asked her the usual questions, almost perfunctorily, and as he talked casually turned over the contents of her basket. He picked up one of the hard-boiled eggs and toyed with it, tossing it a few inches in the air and catching it again.

He glanced up and saw to his surprise a look of alarm on the woman's red face. He went on tossing and catching the egg and the higher he threw it the more disturbed the woman seemed to be. He caught the egg and examined it closely but there was no sign or blemish on the shell, which had a smooth and innocent blankness about it. But he now suspected that there must be something sinister about it, to account for the woman's confusion. Suddenly he cracked it on the edge of her basket and began to peel off the shell. On the white of the egg were microscopic words and marking which were brown in color. When magnified and deciphered, the marks proved to be a plan of the French sector with the identities of the various divisions and bri-

16

gades that occupied it. The peasant woman was inevitably tried and executed as a spy.

The Germans had hit on the ingenious fact that if one writes in acetic acid on the shell of an egg and, after the acid dries, boils the egg, the writing will be absorbed through onto the white and will leave no trace, either to the naked eye or even to a powerful microscope, on the outside of the shell. It was sheer accident that the Counter-Intelligence Service should have discovered this or, perhaps I should say in fairness to the officer concerned, accident plus the knowledge of practical psychology which roused his suspicions the moment the peasant woman appeared confused. But once the method was broken the Germans should have stopped it in spite of its ingenuity. With their one failing as enemies, however, the love of routine with its corresponding lack of initiative, they persevered with the same trick long after they must have been aware that the Counter-Intelligence knew of it and had circulated the information. I am personally aware of three cases in the Second World War in which this trick was used and broken. There must have been many other occasions, unknown to me, where a German agent was needlessly sacrificed through the routine-mindedness of his superiors.

Those, then, are the ten main attributes which the potential spy-catcher must possess. Enthusiasm is obviously not enough. The interested reader might like to examine his qualifications for the job by marking himself out of a total of ten marks on each factor. Anyone who could honestly place himself with over 75 marks out of a possible 100

17

should get in touch with M.I.5 without delay. A man like that could be of immense use to his country. But I doubt whether one person in a hundred thousand would really qualify. To that person I should add the warning note that, given these qualifications, it would still take at least five years of training to make him an efficient Counter-Intelligence agent.

Toward the end of this book I propose to devote some pages to discussing counterespionage in the light of postwar developments. I need only stress here briefly that it is too late to build up or expand an efficient spy-catching organization once a war has broken out. To choose the right men and to train them takes many years to achieve.

I now come on to one of the more controversial aspects of my theme—the place of women in Counter-Intelligence work. Some readers may have noticed that so far I have always spoken of spy-catchers in the masculine sense. It is my own view, backed up by thirty years of experience, that women either as spies or as spy-catchers are on the whole quite useless. I am no woman-hater in principle. I like women—in their right place. But apart from "Mademoiselle le Docteur" in the First World War, there has never been a woman spy or a woman spy-catcher to compete with the best men in the same field. Mata Hari certainly won fame and gave her name to the public's conception of the glamorous female spy, but she was a stupid, impulsive creature and had she not been executed and thus martyred would never have been remembered. Let me try to substantiate these remarks.

18

At one stage in the last war I was helping to train secret agents who were to be parachuted into Occupied Europe. Several Dutch women who had escaped from Holland came to see me and pleaded to be allowed to volunteer for this dangerous job. They were obviously sincere and deeply patriotic. To each one I would say, "What risks are you prepared to take?"

Each would invariably reply, simply and without false heroics, "I am prepared to give my life for my country."

My automatic answer was, "That is the last thing we want. Dead, you are useless to us. But are you prepared to go on living and to give your body?"

This was a question duty made me ask but never without a sense of disgust. It was the crux of the matter. Most women have three inherent failings where spying is concerned. One is that of necessity they lack the technical knowledge and training. If, for example, it is necessary to find out the details of a new secret engine which the enemy is developing, a garage mechanic starts with more advantages than the most intelligent woman. From his job he already knows the background, whereas most women will have to start from scratch and first of all learn the component parts and the principles of motor power. Where military secrets are concerned, few women know, as men do, the various ranks and the subunits, units, brigades. divisions and so forth that make up the modern army. Such knowledge can, of course, be acquired. But it takes up valuable time which could be better spent in more important learning.

Secondly, women are more conspicuous than men in unusual surroundings. A man, dressed up as a laborer, may spend hours near a lonely gun site, for instance, without his presence being remarked on. But a woman, especially if she is young and pretty, will draw attention to herself at once and will probably attract what our American friends refer to as "wolf whistles." Again, a man can enter a dockside bar in a seaport and, suitably dressed, he will be taken for granted. A woman would at once be out of place. Thus her very appearance limits a woman spy's movements and so limits her value as an agent.

Thirdly, and this is the most important factor, most women's control over their emotions is more unreliable than that of men. I risk a storm of abuse from my women readers in suggesting this but experience has taught me that it is true. I have known two or three cases of women, German, British and French, who were set the task of gaining the affections of some senior officer on the other side. This they did only too successfully and then spoiled everything by falling genuinely in love with their victims. The logical step followed. They went over to the enemy and betrayed all the training and the secrets which they had acquired from their own country's Intelligence Service. I have known male spies who became renegades but never for such a reason. A spy has no room for a soft heart.

In my opinion the only limited use a woman spy has is to gain information for her country by seducing a senior officer or official on the other side and subsequently blackmailing him into giving further information by threatening to report him to his security officers or, worse still perhaps, to his wife. That is why I always asked the Dutch women who volunteered for spy work whether they were prepared to give their bodies for their country. This is something that the average decent woman could not do in cold blood. A woman who would be prepared to sleep with a stranger, often a physically repulsive stranger, in order to worm secrets out of him needs the soul of a harlot. And harlots are notoriously unreliable. Thus, as potential spies, women do not rate very high in my opinion. Nor do they make good spy-catchers. Many a husband who, arriving home late, has come to dread his wife's detailed catechism, may violently disagree with me on this score. Yet in thirty years' experience in which I have met, or studied the tactics of, the leading exponents of Intelligence and Counter-Intelligence work in Europe and America, I have never come across a woman, with the one exception perhaps of "Mademoiselle le Docteur," who shone at either branch.

CHAPTER II

Methods of Interrogation

1

THERE are several ways of extracting information from a suspect. Before discussing the methods which I personally have evolved, through a process of trial and error, I should like to mention briefly methods used both in England and elsewhere. In Nazi Germany physical torture was widely used; the methods varied with the ingenuity of the interrogator from straightforward whipping to thumbscrews, the removal of finger- and toenails without anesthetic and the breaking of limbs or the tightening of a metal band by slow degrees around the suspect's head. A dentist's drill, particularly when it began to bite down into the sensitive nerves under the tooth, also proved a highly effective weapon. The Soviet Russian methods are not easy to calculate exactly, because few political prisoners have lived to tell the story of their interrogation and fewer still have managed to slip through the chinks in the Iron Curtain. It is reasonable to surmise, however, that the Russian M.V.D. relies to a great extent on underfeeding and drugs to weaken a prisoner's resistance, coupled with long and intensive interrogations sometimes lasting thirty-six hours

22

without a break. The suspect is then returned to his cell, drops at once into the deep sleep of utter exhaustion and, an hour later, is waked up for further interrogation. Continued lack of sleep breaks the resistance of the strongest and most stubborn person. Methods used in the United States vary from the "grilling" of the "third degree" in which a suspect may be questioned for many hours under a powerful light by relays of interrogators, to the use of the supposedly reliable scientific aids such as the "truth drug" and the lie detector. I say "supposedly reliable" as I personally do not believe in the infallibility of either. An injection of the truth drug or, as it is properly named, pentathol puts the suspect's conscious mind to sleep and his nonconscious mind will cause him to blurt out the truth. Or so its exponents claim. Having experimented, I have discovered that years of practice can enable one to train one's subconscious mind to the extent of restraining speech under an anesthetic. The lie detector is an ingenious mechanism based on the theory that a person's metabolic rate alters under the stress of emotion, which is scientifically proved. The exponents of this method go further and state that it can be applied to tell whether the person being interrogated is speaking the truth or is lying. I am prepared to admit that the theory has statistics on its side but not that it is one hundred per cent effective. From experience I have found a few resolute, cool-headed men who can outwit the lie detector. Only a few, but they are sufficient. For evidence of this nature to be admitted in a court of justice there must be no exceptions to the general rule.

Nazi Germany, Soviet Russia and the United States, as far as its "third degree" methods are concerned, rely to a great extent on physical hardship to get the information required from a suspect. There is no doubt that physical torture will ultimately break any man, however strong in body or determined in mind. I knew one incredibly brave man who fell into the hands of the Gestapo and who had all his fingernails and toenails forcibly extracted and one leg broken without uttering a word of useful information. But he himself admitted that he was at the end of his resistance. It so happened that his torturers were baffled and gave up at that stage. Had they gone on, even with some minor discomfort compared to the exquisite agony he had so far suffered, he would have broken and confessed all.

No man could stand up indefinitely to the water torture. This is the simple and ancient method of allowing a tap to drip at several seconds' interval on a man's head. This, I am convinced, would break a strong man in a matter of minutes and make a raving lunatic of any human being after an hour.

Apart from its inherent loathsomeness and the fact, for which we may devoutly thank God, that evidence extracted under duress is not admissible in a British court of law, physical torture has one overwhelming disadvantage. Under its spur an innocent man will often confess to some crime he has never committed, merely to gain a respite. If he has been badly tortured, he will even invent a crime involving the death penalty, preferring quick death to a continuation of his agony. Physical torture will ultimately

24

make any man talk but it cannot ensure that he will tell the truth.

It is a known fact that in time of war agents on active service are given three different kinds of pill to carry always on them. One kind is the "knockout drops," which would render a man unconscious for twenty-four hours. Another is the Benzedrine pill, which stimulates a tired person into further bursts of mental energy. The third is the suicide pill; it is composed of cyanide or some other equally deadly and quick-acting poison. Each of these different kinds of pill has its uses, and the last-named in particular is for the agent who realizes that he is about to be captured and who knows that he cannot stand up to the ensuing torture. It is a brave man who can carry his own death around with him in the shape of a tiny pill and who will make use of it rather than give away vital information.

That is all I wish to say on the methods of physical torture for extracting information. Such methods are usually effective but clumsy and utterly repugnant to civilized people. They are also a confession of weakness. The interrogator is prepared to admit from the outset that his suspect is mentally superior and will thus write off his chances of outwitting his suspect through verbal questioning.

The Deuxième Bureau, the former French equivalent to the British M.I.5, under which I received all my early training, had an ingenious method which usually produced results. Two interrogators were allotted to each suspect. One of them would be the bullying type, always shouting, threatening and thumping the table with his fist. The other would be the quiet, sympathetic type, apparently on the prisoner's side and doing his best to restrain his violent colleague. The interrogation would reach a crescendo with the "bully" shouting abuse and making the most fearsome threats, when he would be suddenly called away on some official pretext. The "sympathetic" interrogator would then continue the questioning in a mild and friendly way, perhaps offering the suspect a cigarette and soothing his fears. The sudden change in atmosphere nearly always produced results, and out of relief or relaxation of the tension the suspect soon found himself blurting out a full confession.

Scotland Yard usually goes in for the method of sympathy by itself. Their detectives are adept at producing the "all friends together" kind of atmosphere which implies that, after all, people are only human and are bound to make mistakes. Their detectives are polite, friendly and understanding—and very efficient at obtaining freely given confessions. As a Dutchman who has spent many years in England, I am perhaps privileged to put off the self-depreciation and modesty of the average Englishman and say that these methods of sympathy with the suspect spring from the essential tolerance and the wish to give the hunted a sporting chance which are characteristic of England. Unlike many other judicial systems, the accused in a British court of law starts off with the priceless advantage that the onus of proof lies with the prosecution. This is also implicit in all the stages that lead from his arrest to his appearance in court. British officialdom frowns on the suggestion that any advantage may be taken over a prisoner before his trial or information extracted from him by threats or duress. Many readers will recall the case of the brigadier in a south-coast town during the war. A Nazi airman who had been shot down after machine-gunning the streets of the town was brought before the brigadier and was both arrogant and offensive. The latter, momentarily enraged by his attitude and realizing that the airman had only just been shooting at defenseless women and children, struck him with his cane. The brigadier was court-martialed and dismissed from the Service. It seems a heavy penalty for one impulsive blow struck under extreme provocation but, on reflection, one realizes the important principle behind it.

A more humorous case happened to me in 1941. I had been interrogating a suspect, who was later proved guilty of espionage, and during the course of my questioning I called the man a liar—which he undoubtedly was. I happened to be overheard and was later summoned into the presence of a very senior Home Office official who gave me a lecture on the enormity of my offense. The interrogation had taken place on Home Office property and there appears to be a strict Home Office ruling that no suspect may be called an outright liar. The interrogator may paraphrase the remark by saying to the suspect, "I suggest that your answer to my last question contained certain inaccuracies," or words to that effect, but he may not insult the poor victim or injure his feelings by calling him a plain unvarnished liar! At the time I was both amused and a little irritated, because my so-called victim had been a particularly loathsome creature as well as a brazen liar of the first

27

order. Looking back, I realize that this Home Office ruling, although perhaps a little exaggerated in its application, was nevertheless on the right lines; but I must confess that there were occasions during my career when circumstances made it seem unwise for me to adhere to such a ruling.

After the liberation of Holland part of my duties was to train many young Dutchmen for the Counter-Intelligence Service. At this time I was working under the pseudonym of Frank Jackson. The notes for one of the series of lectures I drew up are reproduced at the end of this chapter. They deal exclusively with my methods of interrogation. I need not therefore say much about them here. There is, however, one point I should like to stress. My object in any cross-examination was always a simple one. It was to provoke in the suspect an emotional crisis as early as possible in the course of questioning. The reason for that is not hard to find. A cross-examination is primarily a battle of wits and one side or the other must grasp the initiative early in the game and then retain it. The interrogator starts at a natural advantage. He has nothing to fear, except failure, and even then it will not prove fatal to him. He can conduct the interrogation when and where he likes and can decide when it is to be broken off and when resumed. But he will lose the advantages inherent in the situation if he does not put them to good use by getting his opponent rattled early in the questioning. If he can make the suspect angry or frightened by his questions he will have taken a long stride toward success; and here, of course, is where a knowledge of practical psychology, the ability to work on a suspect's

28

emotions and to size him up accurately and without delay, plays its important role.

Although they would never stoop to physical torture, some Counter-Intelligence officers have been known to use physical discomfort as an aid. They have given the suspect a hard chair to sit on or have made him stand to attention for long periods of questioning. One quite common trick, used I believe by interrogators in the Army when they were dealing with a senior enemy officer who might be an easy victim to embarrassment, was to offer him large quantities of tea or coffee before the interrogation and then to prolong the questions until the needs of nature were pressing him to such an extent that he would often give away vital information in order to be free to relieve himself. Personally, I strongly deprecate such methods. True, they do not actually constitute physical torture. But they are close to the borderline and may occasionally stray over it.

It may be quixotic but I have always tried to start level with the suspect. He may sit in a comfortable chair if he wishes to; he may loll back if he prefers. The hours set for questioning must not be so excessive as to strain his endurance. They might be from nine in the morning to six in the evening with an hour's break for lunch. Above all, I would expect to conduct the whole interrogation myself and not rely on snatching a rest while a substitute questioner carried on in my place. Nor, as I have mentioned previously, would I take notes during the cross-examination. My intention would be to break down the official atmosphere and get on familiar terms with the suspect, unless I felt he was more likely to be impressed by official severity. And always in my mind would be the thought of seizing the initiative by provoking him into an emotional crisis. Often, if all else failed and I strongly suspected that my man was a spy although his story appeared to be water-tight, I would get him to repeat it over and over again, from beginning to end, each time without omitting a single detail. This repetition might take a week, working normal hours, and would be a supreme test for both his patience and mine—and of our memories. Sooner or later, if he was not genuine, he would trip up over some minor detail and then the door to his ultimate disclosure would be slightly ajar. Once I had got a foot inside that door, I was on the way to success.

2

I should now like to sketch in brief the background against which interrogations took place in the Second World War. Conditions were far more difficult then than they had been when the First World War broke out. By a piece of luck and by shrewd judgment every German spy operating in England was rounded up and arrested within twenty-four hours of the outbreak of war in August, 1914. Karl Lody, the first German spy to arrive after hostilities began, was already expected and was caught with the great-est ease. This story has often been told and I need not enlarge on it except by giving the outlines. In 1911 during a German state visit to London, a high-ranking attaché made a habit of visiting a barbershop in the Caledonian

Road. This was not the kind of establishment to which a senior Prussian officer would normally go for a haircut and the suspicions of the Counter-Intelligence Service were at once aroused. A watch was kept on the shop and all letters reaching and leaving it were examined. Counter-Intelligence soon realized that the shop was the "post office" for the German espionage system in England. Wisely our authorities did not disclose their knowledge at this stage but merely kept a close watch and a full dossier on the activities radiating from the barbershop. As soon as war was declared they struck and in one blow destroyed the whole espionage system so carefully built up over three years. It was a grave setback for the German Intelligence which never managed to repair the damage during the rest of the war. All because a senior German officer chose an insufficiently aristocratic neighborhood for his haircut.

The Second World War broke out in vastly different and more difficult circumstances for the British Counter-Intelligence system. There is normally a large element of foreigners in London and the other big cities, which might be friendly to the country's enemies. From the early nineteen-thirties onward this element had been swollen by thousands of refugees from Germany and Italy, most of them violently antagonistic to Hitler and Mussolini and many of them having fled on this account. But it was always possible for the Nazis and Fascists to have taken advantage of circumstances and slipped several spies in among the genuine refugees. There were also some Englishmen who sympathized politically with the Nazi methods or

31

who genuinely believed that we should avoid war by siding with Hitler.

Under Defense Regulation 18B the major suspects were interned when war broke out, but however wide the net was flung the meshes were not close enough to catch all the fish. One of the ironic tragedies of total war is that the liberty of the individual, the mainspring of a country's will to fight against an aggressor, is the first casualty. Many sincere patriots were opposed to the framing of Regulation 18B and there is no doubt that several innocent men and women were caught in it. For example, von Rintelen, the celebrated "dark invader" of the First World War, who was a vehement hater of Hitler and his ways and who was later proved to be completely genuine, spent the greater part of 1941 and 1942 interned in Chelsea. I got to know him quite well during that time, and he could never understand why the country he wanted to help and which would have profited greatly from his vast experience of German spying should treat him so churlishly. It is the old story of the omelette and the eggs. One cannot make war without breaking certain principles—which is one of the major disasters of a war.

As soon as the 1939 war broke out the many thousands of German refugees who had been arriving for several years in England had to be "screened." This in itself was a major task. After Dunkirk, only a few months later, another 150,000 refugees poured into the country from Denmark, Holland, Norway, France and even from Czechoslovakia and Poland. They presented a grave problem, especially as the evacuation of the B.E.F. and then a possibly imminent invasion had to be prepared for as well. A little later, while the flood of incoming refugees was still in spate, the Luftwaffe air raids began and also complicated the problem. England had its own homeless to look after as well as the refugees from overseas.

The system improvised to deal with the latter was as follows. Five reception centers were set up in London, at Fulham Road, Balham, Bushey Park, the Crystal Palace and Norwood. The centers were organized by the London County Council and each was run, chosen no doubt with admirable ingenuity, by—a workhouse master! From the security side I was attached to the center at Norwood, which I came to know best of the five centers. It had formerly been a hospital and the buildings were all of the two-floor type. There were no cellars and no air-raid shelters. A wire fence had been hastily erected around the perimeter and was guarded by soldiers.

The increasing batches of refugees often arrived in the small hours of the morning. From June, 1940, their arrival usually coincided with an air raid. Sometimes up to seven hundred of them at a time would reach Norwood in a fleet of London buses. The women and several of the men would already be on the verge of hysteria through the privations of their escape and through worry over the fate of their families. The confusion of arriving in the dark, cold, lonely and hungry, aggravated by the dangers of an air raid to greet them, would often tip the scales and turn them into a bunch of gesticulating and screaming semi-maniacs.

33

Restoring order in the dark among a crowd of complete strangers is not the simplest of tasks. However, somehow or other it would be done and then all the refugees had to be registered and their names and nationalities duly noted. After that a hot drink and some food, and then the problem of finding them a place to sleep and blankets to sleep in for what remained of the night. The semblance of order so painfully won might soon be completely upset by the panic of another Luftwaffe air raid at this point. The German bombers seemed to use a "bomb alley" which lay across Norwood and the Crystal Palace so that either or both centers were certain to get their share of bombs doled out every raid.

By dawn those of us who were in charge at the center, having been up all night, were surely ready for bed. But now our real work began. After the refugees had been given a bath and possibly had both their bodies and their clothes treated for lice, they were each carefully examined by a medical officer. Any with infectious diseases from smallpox to scabies were of course segregated from the rest. Many more might be in need of medical attention after their long and arduous travels.

Then the Counter-Intelligence got to work. The luggage belonging to perhaps seven hundred refugees had to be sorted out and scrupulously examined. Every scrap of paper, the pages of every book, had to be turned over and scrutinized. Clothes had to be searched, including the linings and the seams, and so had all the cases and bags. This was no perfunctory check on the lines of a customs ex-

34

amination. It had to be done with the maximum of close attention. Many refugees in an honest attempt to help the country which gave them shelter would have brought maps, photographs and drawings giving information of the occupying German forces, and all these documents would have to be closely scrutinized.

Once this task was concluded the job of verbal interrogation began. The suspects were weeded out from the obviously genuine and were held for detailed examination.

These processes might take a week during which time all refugees were held incommunicado. They were not allowed to receive letters or get in touch with the outside world until they had been cleared officially by the Counter-Intelligence. Then they were sent to the immigration officer and, after he had issued them the various permits and identity cards, they were officially permitted to "land" in England. Any doubtful refugees—and the number included several genuine people who were unlucky not to have any corroborative evidence to their testimony—were kept on one side still under guard. There was a most efficient Central Register which contained details of all refugees who had arrived. Often it was possible to check a genuine refugee's story through the Central Register and, perhaps, locate a previous arrival who could vouch for the doubtful one's *bona fides*.

This improvised method of screening refugees went on until April, 1941, when a colleague and I were given the task of organizing a special center which became known as the Royal Victoria Patriotic School. It was at Clapham.

35

Guided by the experience gained bitterly through many days and nights of handling refugees at the temporary centers, my colleagues and I managed to found an efficient system through which all refugees passed with the least personal inconvenience to themselves and the tightest security to us. In addition the spate of refugees had now slowed down to a steady stream, and as the numbers of examiners were continually increasing, we were thus able to devote more time and attention to each one. From April, 1941, until October, 1942, when I was transferred to the Dutch Counter-Intelligence Service, I worked exclusively at this institution as head of the examiners. During that time I saw the staff of examiners increase from five to a total of thirty-two.

There is no doubt in my mind that during the first hectic six months or so after the evacuation from Dunkirk some spies could have passed, and probably did pass, undetected through our screen. It was impossible in the confusion and without sufficient numbers of trained interrogators to ensure that every suspicious refugee was put aside. The numbers arriving were too many and the time available for their scrutiny too short to get one hundred per cent results.

Screening refugees in London was not the end of my activities in the days after Dunkirk. After the fall of France the coast of Europe was sealed off by the Germans apart from the tiny strip of Portugal. The only official port of entry into Britain then was Lisbon. Ships from Lisbon called in regularly at Liverpool and Glasgow while sea planes from the same place arrived twice a week at Poole near Bournemouth and land planes at Whitchurch near Bristol. In addition to my duties in London I was given the task of taking a team of examiners to each of these four places in turn to check all incoming arrivals, both British and foreign. It involved many hours of travel up and down the country and I believe I was the only Counter-Intelligence agent to be kept permanently on this job until all my energies had to be devoted to the Royal Victoria Patriotic School at Clapham, to which all arrivals by plane and ship were then sent for examination.

This then was the background from which the following true stories I have to tell emerged. Compared to the 1914 war when all German spies had been located and were quickly rounded up and in which no refugees fled from the Continent, the job of Counter-Intelligence was a difficult one, carried out in difficult circumstances. Just as the B.E.F. was unprepared for the German Panzer assault of May, 1940, so was Counter-Intelligence unprepared for the flood of refugees that swept into the system. And just as the Army had to regroup and learn to beat the Germans at their own national sport, so also had Counter-Intelligence to train itself from its hard-won experience. But with the difference that every mistake might be a big one with far-reaching consequences. For the past five years I have been daily expecting to see the publication in Germany of a book entitled *The Years I Spent Spying in England*, by some German who spent five happy, and to himself profitable, years in this country from 1940 to 1945. So far it has not appeared but I would not be surprised if it did. Unless the potential writer is still under commission and has not yet come above ground?

37

APPENDIX TO CHAPTER II

NOTES ON EXAMINATION

I. EXAMINATION OF PROPERTY

We can never put enough emphasis on the vital importance of a very thorough examination of the property of arrivals.

Before seeing the arrival himself, his property must be examined with minute care and special attention paid to the contents of pocketbooks, diaries, notebooks, and every scrap of writing the man has brought with him.

Any tiny piece of paper, such as a crumpled-up piece of cigarette paper, should be carefully examined.

Anything cryptical should be carefully put aside and an explanation asked for at the end of the first interrogation.

All addresses should be noted and an explanation asked for when interrogating.

If there are any books in the property, special attention should be given to the fly leaves and if they are in paper wrappers, the wrappers should be taken off. If the corner of any page should be turned down, that page should be specially examined, for either marks or any pin pricks.

If there are any dictionaries, turn up the pages on which each new letter starts, and see if there is any marking above or under the new index letter.

Matchboxes should be emptied and examined inside.

Any chemical compound, whether some patent medicine in tablet form or powders, must be inquired into.

38

Keep a special watch for pieces of cotton wool and wooden toothpicks or orange sticks in pocketbooks.

Be especially careful with sheets of carbon paper that have been used, also with sheets of used blotting paper; they may at some future time supply vital evidence.

II. FIRST INTERROGATION

(a) *General*

The first interrogation of any arrival should be not so much an interrogation as the taking of a complete statement in detail by the examinee.

This interrogation should in all cases be conducted with complete courtesy; and at no time should the examiner express by word or mien, any doubt, surprise, or any other human emotion, except perhaps admiration.

Obvious lying or bragging should be encouraged, not squashed.

Contradictions should not be pointed out.

If the examinee is one of a party and others of that party have, during their first interrogation, made statements which are at variance with those of the present examinee, never point out such discrepancies during the first interrogation.

The more doubtful or suspicious a story is, the more the examiner should appear to accept it without any hesitation. No questions or remarks of any kind whatsoever should be made by the examiner which might put the examinee on his guard and lead him to realize that his story is disbelieved.

If, at the finish of his statement, you feel reasonably certain that the story is genuine and that you have to deal with a more or less routine case, you can then begin your cross-examination and put any questions you may think necessary to elucidate and complete the story. If, after these elucidations, you are convinced that the examinee is quite all right and that no sec-

39

ond interrogation is necessary, you can then make a definite recommendation for release.

If, however, you have any doubt on any point of the story, the finish of the statement should at the same time be the finish of the first interrogation.

(b) *Report*

At the beginning of your report, besides the standardized items which have already been laid down, always also include:

(1) the religion of the subject;

(2) whether he ever belonged to any political party or union and if so, to which;

(3) languages and proficiency in same.

At the end of the story, do not begin your recommendation with the phrase that the man makes a good or bad "impression."

Impressions are fatal.

You may take it for granted that the really clever spy will make an excellent impression.

One of the world's most famous criminologists once stated that the person who had made the best impression on him had been a woman who had poisoned her children for the insurance money, and the one who had made the worst impression on him had been a famous philanthropist and reformer.

If you are not satisfied with the story, do not come to a conclusive conclusion.

Specify your doubts and objections, stating your opinion, and if you have a logical explanation which would fit all the facts, give it in detail and recommend holding for further interrogation. If you have not, ask for another opinion.

Look-ups should be asked for immediately after the first interrogation by the examiner himself. It is important not to waste any time in doing so as the results of those look-ups are usually of the greatest help if they are in by the time the second interrogation is held.

III. SECOND INTERROGATION

Before commencing a second interrogation, if the man has been examined for the first time by some other examiner, begin by very carefully studying the report of the first interrogation.

In doing so, however, you must be constantly on your guard against the effects of suggestion, whether intentional or unconscious.

When the facts of a case are set forth by an examiner, they are nearly always presented, consciously or unconsciously, in terms of inference.

Certain facts, which appear to the first examiner to be vital, are recorded with emphasis and in detail, while other facts which he considered to be subordinate or trivial have been partially suppressed.

This assessment of evidential value given by the first examiner should never be accepted by the second.

The whole case must be considered, and each fact weighed separately, and you may find that it will turn out that the leading factor in the case is one that has been almost passed over by the first examiner because he considered it to be practically negligible.

It pays sometimes to lose your temper artificially; NEVER really lose it.

Any critical points should NOT be approached gradually.

The surprise question or statement is to the examinee what the ambush is to the soldier on the field.

Moreover, wherever possible, this surprise attack should not consist of a question but of a statement.

For instance, if you have good reason to believe that the man has been in touch with the German consul in a certain town, do not ask him: "Did you ever visit the German consulate there?" Say instead: "What was the date of your last visit to the German consulate there?"

41

Such a vital question, or better still, implied vital statement, should be made abruptly, apropos of nothing; watch the reaction of your subject's Adam's apple and eyelids.

If there are several doubtful and important points in his story, it is advisable not to deal with them one after the other, but to stagger the cross-examination, frequently shifting, without warning, from one point to the other.

Before starting your cross-examination, make a thorough psychological effort in order to sum up your subject and treat him accordingly.

You can break some men by bullying, on others this has the reverse effect.

Decide beforehand whether you are likely to obtain results with the subject you are dealing with, either by bullying, by sarcasm, by cold and impassive treatment, or by sympathy and by working on his emotions.

The Story within a Story

In many recommendations in first reports, you may find that the first examiner recommends holding the man until a certain point or points in his story, which are either improbable or perhaps even impossible, are cleared up.

In all such cases, you must be strongly on your guard against what I call, for want of a better term, "the story within the story."

The author of any story to be told by an agent on arrival in enemy country will, if he knows his business, always include this story within the story "just in case."

I shall endeavor to give an instance of what I mean:

A sailor is under interrogation. He tells a story of an escape from occupied territory, where for eight months he had been doing nothing because he refused to sail for the Germans and had only been trying to help some secret organization in arranging sabotage, etc. He then escaped and came here via Spain and Portugal.

The story, in itself, sounds feasible and is told with great assurance and self-possession, and the man makes "an excellent impression."

The strange part of the case, however (and this is the reason for the second interrogation), is that this unemployed sailor has come over with fifty pounds in English currency and two hundred American dollars.

How is it that an unemployed sailor has got all this money?

His original reply to this question has been that this money constitutes his savings.

The first examiner, very rightly, does not believe this and his recommendation is to hold the man until this point is elucidated.

This is where the story within the story comes in.

After a considerable amount of pressure and great hesitation, the man says at last, "Well, sir, it is no use trying to deceive you any more; I will tell you the truth. I am a thief."

He then goes on to describe at great length and in full detail, how he robbed a woman who had offered him hospitality for the night, of her jewelry and how he had disposed of same in the black market.

It is a psychological fact that we are apt to accept as true any statement anybody makes against himself, and if the examiner accepts this story, the doubtful point in Report No. 1 is elucidated and, as we are concerned with security only, the case ceases to be of interest and the man may be released.

A good author of stories for people being sent out will never make his man perfect.

There will always be a story within the story, in the background, very much against the character of the man, in order to have it accepted if and when it has to come out, and he will

43

be either a thief, a murderer, a *souteneur*, just for such cases as the instance I have given.

It is against this story within the story that we have to be strongly on our guard; if after a great effort you think you have been successful in breaking a man and he then tells you an item detrimental to himself of this kind, do not accept it as a final solution of the case. On the contrary, register him as a definite suspect.

F. JACKSON

5.9.42

44

CHAPTER III

The Thirteenth Man

1

I⊤ was the first week of September, 1940. Four months earlier the last remnants of the British Expeditionary Force had been evacuated from Dunkirk, leaving the German Wehrmacht on the edge of the Channel. On a clear day their soldiers, lustily singing their favorite song, "Marching against England," could see the misty outlines of the coveted prize across that narrow strip of water, narrow enough for a good swimmer to cross. Only one gigantic stride was required, it seemed, for the all-conquering Wehrmacht with its crack Panzer troops, self-propelled guns and Stuka dive bombers to snatch the one plum that remained beyond its grasp. Hitler himself had supervised the drawing up of his favorite plan—the invasion of England—under the code name of "Operation Sealion."

Air reconnaissance and information from our secret agents on the Continent confirmed the possibilities. Flotillas of barges and small ships were moving into position along the coast between Ostend and Le Havre. One hundred sixty bomber aircraft were transferred from Norway to the Channel area. Short-range dive bombers were spotted on the forward airfields in the Pas de Calais. As Mr. Winston

45

Churchill later wrote in Volume II of his great memoirs: "Moon and tide conditions between the 8th and the 10th (of September) were favourable for invasion on the South-East Coast. . . . The Chiefs of Staff concluded that the possibility of invasion had become imminent."

I had spent the night on duty in my office. Dawn was breaking as I rose, stretched myself and yawned, then went off to shave. I had just returned when a young intelligence officer rushed into the room. He was obviously excited.

"A message for you, sir," he blurted out.

I took the message and held it up to the pale light from the window. The code signature showed that it came from one of our most trusted and resolute agents, who had been left on the Continent to spy for us. The message read: "U-boat departs Zeebrugge tonight 2130 hours carrying 4 spies instructed land England before daylight south coast map reference 432925 these men carefully selected and trained for special mission regarding German Operation Sealion."

I looked up at the excited young man and smiled. "This means business," I said. "Come on, let's get to work."

We consulted a large-scale map of the south coast. There was the spot indicated by the map reference and it had obviously been chosen with care. It was a small secluded cove, and behind it the steep cliffs stood almost sheer, providing cover from inquisitive eyes. But if they would serve to keep the casual observer out they might as easily serve to keep the silent invader in. Manned by resolute watchers, these cliffs could be a death trap for the four spies. The

46

cove was crescent-shaped and far from any village, or even house, if the map were correct. It was wide open to the sea, but there was only one exit on the land side.

I smoked a cigarette while I ran over the simple plan that was forming in my mind. Then I conferred with the Field Security officer, a captain, who had already been detailed to work with me.

"This is how I see it," I said. "The plan is simple, but on a dark night the more simple it is the less likelihood of things going wrong. All we need do is to place men at short intervals along the foot of the cliffs—you see on the map how the beach is funnel-shaped?—and you and I will post ourselves at the neck of the funnel—here. This little path—or track—is the only exit from the beach, short of scaling the cliffs. To go right ashore these four spies have got to get past us."

"How many men will you require, sir?" he asked.

"Let us say a dozen. And have them change into civilian clothes, less conspicuous."

"Armed, of course, sir?"

"Yes, of course. But on no account are they to open fire *without my orders*. That must be strictly understood. We want to get these men alive."

"Yes, sir."

"They must all carry flashlights. We can work out a series of signals before we leave. Any more questions?"

"No, sir."

"Right. We must be in position by midnight. Have your

47

men ready to leave by seven o'clock. That should give us ample time to drive there in comfort."

2

It was growing dusk as we drove along the Great West Road and gradually darkness blotted out the countryside. The blackout on all sides and the feeble beams from our shuttered headlamps gave us the eerie sensation of moving through a strange fourth dimension. The moon had not risen and we felt like ants in a bottle of ink with the cap screwed on. I was chain smoking. Being a heavy smoker, I knew the coming torment of perhaps six hours without being able to light up in case the glow of the cigarette end betrayed our position. I was trying to build up a reserve of the nicotine content in my blood stream and in the darkness smiled at this fantasy. From time to time I glanced at the luminous dial of my watch. We were making good progress and at this rate would easily be in position by the appointed hour.

As I peered out into the blackness of the passing countryside, a strange fancy seized me. In my mind's eye I could see the outlines of the map fifty miles on either side of the English coast. Two lines were converging, one from the land and one from the sea, on that lonely funnel-shaped cove. But the lines of the cliff edge which I had memorized were no longer funnel-shaped in my imagination. They had become the jaws of a trap. Once we were in position the trap would be ready for springing. I thought for a while of the four spies at this moment huddled in the

U-boat that was nosing its way toward the English coast. What kind of men were they? Fanatic patriots taking the supreme risk for their country? Or trained men carrying out orders instinctively? And then I thought of our Field Security fellows who would man the trap. It suddenly occurred to me that the captain and his men were thirteen in number. Was this to be an unlucky omen?

3

We reached the cliffs at the back of the cove on the stroke of midnight. I quickly ran through the orders with the twelve men and their captain huddled round me, dark, unrecognizable shapes against the dark countryside. Man the foot of the cliffs at equal distances apart, no talking, no smoking, above all, no shooting except in absolute self-defense. The signal if any spy came within tackling distance—three short flashes from the nearest flashlight. There were no questions and, one by one, we threaded our way down the narrow cliff path in silence save the occasional muttered curse as someone tripped over an obstruction. At the foot of the cliff the captain and I watched the men disappear into the darkness on either side of the cliff path. We stood together at the junction of the beach with the path, the neck of the "funnel." We could hear the quiet crunching of the men's footsteps on the sand as they crept into position and then silence.

Silence—except for the monotonous ripple of the tide on the beach and the sucking noise it made on the ebb. Ripple and suck, ripple and suck, as it had done from time im-

49

memorial. Tonight the time seemed immemorial and the minutes crawled away. After what felt like a whole night of waiting I was surprised to hear a distant clock in a village church chime the hour of one. Only one o'clock! I turned up my greatcoat collar, plunged my hands deeper in my pockets and hunched up my shoulders against the damp cold of the beach. I ached with all my being for a cigarette. Once when my hand brushed against the packet, I was sorely tempted. But no! the flicker of a match and the red glow of the cigarette end would have been seen miles off to sea, especially if, as I suspected, keen eyes were already scanning the shore through binoculars.

Two o'clock crept toward us, arrived and then receded as slowly. Then three o'clock. I checked my watch with the village church chimes at three o'clock and, what might have been half an hour later, glanced at it again. Only five past three. I held it to my ear but it ticked away steadily. I was too fast in my impatience, not the watch too slow.

It was nearly four o'clock. I turned to the captain and whispered, "I wish to God the blighters would . . ."

Suddenly I saw flashes—one, two, three short jabs of light against the black cliff side. Another torch flashed out, and then another and another. A prowling figure was silhouetted against the shifting beams. As two other flashlights cut beams into the darkness, a second and a third figure could be observed, immobilized by surprise. A light went out suddenly and I could hear the sound of a scuffle. The ring of torchlight closed in and there was a moment of confusion, of shouting and boots plunging in the soft sand.

The captain and I rushed to the center of the confusion and as we arrived, order returned. There were our twelve men triumphant with their dumfounded and dejected captives. As I had the prisoners lined up, I thought to myself, "It is almost too easy." I counted them, one, two, three. It had been too easy. The fourth man was missing.

4

I was certain in my own mind that the message had been correct in mentioning four men. A spy who risks his life in getting a vitally important radio message out of enemy-held territory makes sure that his details are right. Four men, the message had said, and four men there were going to be. But now that the element of surprise was lost, finding the fourth man would be almost impossible before daylight. He could be lying up somewhere between the sea and the cliffs and only the luckiest beam from a torch or the accident of actually stumbling over him would betray his hiding place. So far we had made a satisfactory haul but our night's work would be ruined if we allowed one man to slip through our fingers. The fact that we had not caught him at the first opportunity probably meant that he was the most dangerous and cool-headed of the bunch. He could do uncalculable damage, perhaps ruin our chances of defeating the invasion that seemed imminent. There was one reassuring factor. He must still be on the beach. The cliff path had been guarded throughout and that was the only exit.

I turned to the Field Security captain. "Well, there's

51

only one thing for it. We'll have to stick here until daylight and pick him up then. In the meantime, let's see what we have hooked."

The three men were searched. My admiration for German thoroughness rose by a few degrees. Each of the prisoners was well-dressed in an English suit obviously cut by an English tailor and carrying a well-known London tailor's label. They had plenty of English money in notes of small denomination. They even had the proper identity cards, colored gray for aliens and duly filled in and stamped. Each one carried a compact but powerful radio transmitter.

I ordered the three to be moved sufficiently far apart to be out of earshot of each other and then began to question them. The first two I interrogated were Germans, named Waldberg and Meyer. Like many Germans, although resolute under fire, they offered little resistance when they knew the game was up. They answered all my questions sullenly but in detail.

Before I had spoken to the third man, he broke out in English with, "Could I have a word with you, please, sir?" In surprise I flashed a light in his face. He stood there blinking. I studied him. His accent was marked but it was not a German accent. He was obviously frightened.

"Well?" I said.

And then the story came tumbling out. He was not a German but a Dutchman. He was not really a spy; in fact he was glad to be caught so soon. It saved him the trouble of giving himself up at the nearest police station he could

52

find. He had been too smart for the Germans. He had fooled them into thinking he wanted to be a spy in England, when all the time his one aim was to get over to England and enlist on the side of the Allies. He gave an ingratiating grin as he ended.

It was not the first time I had heard this kind of story but my disgust did not grow less. I can admire an honest spy who risks his life and accepts the consequence of capture with courage. But this glib cowardice was only contemptible. To save his own skin the man would cheerfully betray his comrades. He might, nevertheless, be useful to us.

"All right, you say you are on our side. How many of you came ashore tonight?"

"Four, sir."

"You are absolutely certain there were four of you."

"Yes, sir. Myself, Waldberg, Meyer and Van der Kieboom, sir. That makes the four."

"Van der Kieboom. That's not a German name."

"No, sir. He is Dutch—like me."

So that was established. There really had been four and the message was correct. But where was Van der Kieboom? Perhaps daylight would tell.

5

And so our vigil continued. Five o'clock and then six o'clock came and went. At last, when the night seemed never ending, a streak of pale light showed on the horizon and crept across the still sea toward us. Soon it was possible

53

to distinguish rocks from men and a quarter of an hour later there was enough light to begin the last search.

Our men fanned out in a line and, starting from one end of the beach, slowly paced toward the other. There was gorse and undergrowth, thorny bushes and sand hollows, but every inch of the ground was searched in the half light before the dawn. The Field Security captain and I stood back and watched them gradually making their way forward, bending down under every bush, moving all objects that might afford cover. They were a third of the way along the beach, then halfway, then three-quarters. And then they converged at the far end empty-handed. There was no trace of Van der Kieboom.

I swore out loud, then shouted to them to retrace their steps. The line fanned out again as they returned toward us, searching the ground as meticulously as before. This was fantastic. Van der Kieboom had to be on the beach. Wild thoughts flashed through my mind. Could he have swum back to the U-boat when he heard his comrades captured? But no, there had been no sound of splashing from the sea except the ripple and suck of the monotonous tide. Could he have scaled the cliffs? A glance upward assured me that not even a mountain goat could have ascended in the dark without at least dislodging stones and boulders to give its position away. So Van der Kieboom must still be on the beach. But where?

I clenched my fists in my exasperation and watched the approaching line of searchers. It was now light enough to see the white blur of each face but not to recognize the

54

owner. I looked along the line from right to left and then back again. Suddenly the solution hit me and I laughed aloud. "Clever devil," I said.

The captain looked startled. "What's the matter, sir?"

"What a clever devil," I repeated and then raised my voice. "All right, you men, halt where you are." They halted. I turned to the captain. "Will you come with me? I'm going to introduce you to our friend."

The captain and I strolled along the line of searchers, pausing long enough to recognize each one. Eight, nine, ten. We were nearing the end of the line. Eleven, twelve and—we halted and I put a hand on the last man's shoulder. "Good morning, Van der Kieboom," I said. He was the thirteenth man.

6

In the half light and the confusion he might have got away with it, if we had decided to call the search off. He could have brought up the rear of the party climbing the cliff path and then lain low until the cars departed. He was a clever, resolute man.

If it had not been for the fact that exactly twelve men were chosen for the job and that my superstitiousness had caused me to remember this, I should not have counted them mentally as they approached in line through the gray dawn light. On such slender threads does a man's life hang.

Van der Kieboom, Meyer and Waldberg were tried, sentenced to death and executed. It was the only case in the Second World War where trial and execution of three

55

spies simultaneously were carried out. The fourth man, who had turned King's evidence, was kept in an English prison until the end of the war and was then transferred to a Dutch prison. I have never heard what happened to him after that.

Van der Kieboom fought hard at his trial to save his life. He made the passionate plea that he was a misguided youth, led astray against his better judgment. He asked for one more chance—to enlist in the service of the Allies and be sent to the front line, where a soldier's death might retrieve his honor in the eyes of the world, of his country and of his mother. But his plea was in vain.

He was a convinced and fanatical Nazi. In his last letter written to his mother on the eve of his execution he begged her forgiveness for the pain and sorrow his death would cause her. "If only you hadn't known, Mother," he wrote, "then I would be the happiest and proudest of men in dying for the Great Cause and my Führer." In the will he drew up at the same time he directed his mother to sell his property, his camera and binoculars and all his prized possessions, and forward the proceeds to the German Red Cross if it were possible.

Yes, he was a fanatical Nazi and paid the supreme penalty. But he was also a cool and resourceful man who was captured only because one of the search party happened to be superstitious.

CHAPTER IV

The Spy Who Was Too Thorough

1

Most Germans have a mania for *Gründlichkeit* which can be translated as "thoroughness" or, more loosely, "the art of taking pains." The saying goes that this is equivalent to genius, but in my experience it has occasionally caused a man's death if it is carried to excess. Here is a case where thoroughness went too far.

Alphons Louis Eugene Timmermans was a Belgian, aged thirty-seven and unmarried. He was a merchant seaman and looked a typical sailor. A bluff, straightforward kind of man, with blue eyes and fair, unruly hair. Neatly dressed, capable with his hands, not very intelligent but with plenty of common sense. You could meet a hundred more like him in any seaport in the world.

His story was no more unusual in those stirring times than his appearance. After the Germans occupied Belgium he had decided to make his way to England and join the Free Belgian Merchant Navy, then centered on the port of Brixham. He had traveled alone through Occupied France into the Vichy Zone and, moving always southward, reached the Pyrenees. Being able to look after himself, as any good sailor usually can, he managed to get across the mountain barrier into Spain, where for his pains he was flung into jail. He spent several months in a filthy cell in Barcelona until the Belgian consulate, after making energetic efforts on his behalf, managed to effect his release. From Barcelona he was sent to Lisbon in Portugal where the Belgian consulate there added his name to the lengthening list of refugees awaiting passage to England. Timmermans, young, strong and able to do work of national importance, was given some priority. He reached England in April, 1942, and was sent to the Royal Victoria Patriotic School at Clapham for formal clearance.

Being a Belgian and apparently quite a straightforward case, Timmermans was assigned to a Belgian security officer, who happened to be one of my pupils. Up to this point I had not been personally associated with his case. I was busy at the time with a stubborn Spanish Falangist who was troublesome enough. Clearing Timmermans appeared to be a matter of routine, and in any case the Belgian security officer, being keen, intelligent and hard working, was perfectly capable of dealing with matters of this nature.

As mentioned earlier, at the Royal Victoria Patriotic School we stressed the importance of searching with the utmost care all luggage and personal belongings brought in by refugees. This was usually done after they had made their preliminary statements and before they were given a detailed interrogation, which might well be based on clues picked up from the search of their effects. Even the completely innocent might carry, unknown to themselves,

58

picture postcards, local newspapers and scraps of paper which would yield interesting information to the trained searcher. And the guilty, who came with the purpose of spying, would need to bring the means of communicating the intelligence they obtained. It would be unlikely, of course, that a spy would openly carry a radio transmitter as part of his luggage but he might have hidden away some smaller object, like the microcamera already mentioned. Furthermore, few spies had memories sufficiently retentive to carry the names and addresses, often in a language unfamiliar to them, to which they would have to transmit the information they picked up.

The Royal Victoria Patriotic School contained a large room which was empty of furniture except for a long bare table with chairs drawn up on either side of it. We called it "the lumber room." Every morning examiners would sit at the table with the belongings of their "clients" spread in front of them. They would examine, sometimes under a powerful magnifying glass, the suitcases, briefcases, wallets, pocketbooks, correspondence, fountain pens, spectacle cases, tobacco pouches, cigarette cases, bunches of keys and all the other paraphernalia carried by the refugees. Once passed, the articles would be pushed to one side. The room used to look like a cross between a customs examination and the vicarage jumble sale.

On this bright April morning with the sun shining on the gay flowers tossing in the garden outside, I happened to be sitting at the long table next to the Belgian security officer who was conducting the Timmermans case. I was

59

deep in thought, studying the belongings of my stubborn Spaniard, when the Belgian turned to me and said, "What do you make of this, sir?"

I frowned at having my concentration broken and looked up. He had been systematically emptying the compartments in a shabby, black wallet and had taken out a small envelope. As he held it open, I could see it contained a whitish powder. I was annoyed and spoke abruptly. "How the hell should I know? I'm not a walking laboratory. Send it for analysis and ask for a rush report."

I turned back to my own work and went on looking at the Spaniard's belongings. A minute or two went by and then a timid voice at my elbow asked, "I'm very sorry, sir, but could I interrupt you again?"

I swung round, about to deliver a lecture to young incompetents who could not get on with their own work and let their seniors get on with theirs. And then I saw what he was holding up in his hand. It was a small bunch of orange sticks, such as women use for pushing back the cuticle around their fingernails.

"Good God!" I exclaimed.

"What's the matter, sir?"

"Matter—nothing's the matter. Go on now, show me the cotton wool."

"Cotton wool?" It was his turn to be amazed. The look that flashed across his face betrayed his suspicion that one of us had suddenly taken leave of his senses—and that one was not himself. Nevertheless, he carried out the order and dutifully delved into the next compartment of the wallet.

60

He was dumfounded. His groping fingers pulled out a wad of cotton wool, about three square inches in size. And in that action he sealed the fate of yet another German spy.

2

Explaining the importance of his discovery, I told him to leave the Timmermans case to me and go on with his next case. I sat there for a moment, musing on the *Gründlichkeit*, the German thoroughness, that had betrayed Timmermans. Whoever had briefed him for his trip to England had covered every detail, even the most minute and insignificant. But in so doing that spymaster, whom we learned afterward stayed at the boarding house of the notorious "Aunt Seele" in Lisbon, had given the tyro away just as effectively as if he had written to Counter-Intelligence in advance and warned them of Timmermans' arrival. He had armed him with the three essentials for invisible writing, pyramidon powder to be dissolved in a mixture of water and alcohol, orange sticks as writing instruments and cotton wool to wrap round the point of the stick and thus avoid telltale scratches on the surface of the paper. The pity of it all, from Timmermans' point of view, was that he could have bought any or all of the three essentials at any chemist's shop in England without a question being asked. Now, because his mentor had been too thorough, he was going to have some explaining to do.

3

I knew, however, that it was one thing to realize his guilt and another to get him to admit it. There had to be

61

proof that would stand up in a court of law. His head was inside the noose but it was not yet pulled tight.

I went back to my room and rang for my secretary. I asked her to type out a list of every item of Timmermans' property, omitting nothing however negligible it might appear. Before long the typed list lay on my desk and among the other items the three important ones were clearly included:

> one envelope, containing powder
> one bunch of orange sticks
> one piece of cotton wool.

I had to get Timmermans to admit that these three items belonged to him. In my experience it had occasionally happened—in fact it once happened to me—that a guilty man had sworn that incriminating evidence had been planted on him by his interrogators. With no actual proof to the contrary, his story had been upheld by the judge and he had gone free. I had learned my lesson. It was not going to happen twice to me, if I could avoid it. I sent for Timmermans.

He came into the room with his slightly rolling walk and sat down, when invited to do so. He looked straight into my eyes and smiled a shy, but quite unself-conscious smile. I smiled back and held out my cigarette case. He took a cigarette which I lit for him. He inhaled and sat back at his ease.

"Well, Timmermans," I said, in Flemish, "yours is luckily a straightforward case. No complications. Naturally

62

we've checked on your story and find it perfectly in order."

He smiled again.

"They tell me you are keen to join the Free Belgian Merchant Navy and do your bit," I went on.

"Yes, sir—very keen." His smile was enthusiastic.

"I was glad to hear that. The Belgian Merchant Navy needs good men like you." I turned over some papers. "Well, there doesn't seem to be any need to keep you longer. Everything's in order and you'll want to join your fellow countrymen as soon as you can. I'll ask the immigration officer to land you at once. With any luck you'll catch a train for Brixham tonight. How's that?"

"That's splendid, sir. Thank you very much." His grin now spread almost from ear to ear.

"There's just one thing," I added. "Only a formality. Here are your belongings," I pointed to them spread out on the desk, "and here is a list of them. It's the official receipt. Would you mind checking each item of your property against the list and then, if you're satisfied that nothing is missing, perhaps you would sign the receipt. Then you can take your property and be on your way."

He took the list from me, and went through it. "Everything in order, sir," he said.

I took out my fountain pen; and passed it across the table. There was silence in the room except the scratching of the pen as Timmermans signed his death warrant.

He pushed back his chair. "Is that all, sir?" he asked.

"Not quite." Opening his wallet I slowly removed the powder, the orange sticks and the cotton wool, lining them

63

neatly on the blotting pad. I stared at him the whole time. He went pale and the smile faded. One eyelid twitched.

"Before you go, perhaps you will explain why you happen to be carrying these particular articles in your wallet. Articles that you admit are yours by the list you've just signed."

He gulped and looked at the list in my hand, almost as though he were sizing the distance between us for an opportunity to snatch that damning piece of paper away from me. Then he relaxed and the shadow of his former smile twisted his lips.

"Of course I can explain, sir. For a moment you had me puzzled but I remember it clearly now. When I was in prison at Barcelona—they told you about that, didn't they, sir?—I shared a cell with a Spanish Communist. Early one morning the guards came to fetch him away. As we heard their footsteps in the corridor outside, he passed those three things on to me. Said he'd be shot if they were found on him. He asked me to keep them until he came back." An expressive shrug. "Well, he never did come back. I just put those things in my wallet and forgot all about them until this minute. Honest, sir."

I hid my admiration for this quick reply and just looked at him. There was only one way to break him down, I thought. I tried it. I smiled, like a man beginning to see a good joke, and the smile broadened. My shoulders shook as if I were suppressing my laughter and then a chuckle broke out, followed by another and another. I flung my head back and roared with mirth until I was red in the face

64

and the tears streamed from my eyes. Nothing in life, it seemed, was as funny as this exquisite joke.

Timmermans sat rigid with teeth clenched. A vein on his forehead throbbed and his knuckles showed as white blotches. Then he began to tremble as my shrieks of laughter rang out. At last he broke. Pressing his palms against his ears, he sprang up, shouting and cursing, pleading with me to stop my insane laughter. "I'll tell you everything," he screamed, "but for God's sake stop laughing."

Two hours later, having been warned that anything he said would be taken down and might be used as evidence, he had dictated and signed a complete confession which, neatly typed, lay on my desk.

He was hanged at Wandsworth Prison on July 7, 1942, a victim of *Gründlichkeit*.

CHAPTER V

The Phantom Refugees

1

IT ALL started in Soho, that strange area northeast of Piccadilly Circus where one can usually find the best food and the worst criminals in London. Two police constables on their beat late one night happened to stop three odd-looking men who were begging and, following the usual wartime routine, asked to see their identity cards. They had no identity cards. The three beggars could only speak French and the policemen could only speak English. With the ponderous courtesy associated with British law and order, the policemen suggested that the three should accompany them to Cannon Row Police Station. They "went quietly."

The inspector on duty there knew enough French to interrogate the three men after a fashion. The story which he pieced together was a disturbing one. It was then the late summer of 1941, and although Operation Sealion, Hitler's plan for the invasion of England, had not taken place the year before, it was still on the cards. During the breathing space the coastal defenses had been hurriedly organized. Rusty coils of barbed wire sprouted along the sandy beaches and rocky coves around the coast of Britain.

66

Mines had been planted at all obvious landing places for vehicles. Concrete road blocks and tank traps could be seen along every road capable of carrying tanks. General Montgomery, with his great victories still before him, but already noted for his personality and Spartan methods of training his troops, commanded the Twelfth Corps in the southeast of England, where the first brunt of an invasion might have to be borne. All around the shores of Britain there were dawn and dusk stand-tos; patrols and lookouts scanned the beaches and the sea for signs of the coming enemy.

No wonder then that the police inspector was perturbed by the three men's story. They claimed to have escaped from France a few days earlier in a boat, had landed on the northeast coast of England in broad daylight without being spotted and had hitchhiked to London through several prohibited areas. They had not been stopped at any road block nor questioned at any time nor asked to prove their identity until the two police constables had halted them a few minutes before.

Two alternatives came to the inspector's mind—and both were equally disturbing. If the men's story was true then the defenses of Great Britain were in no fit shape to stop a German invasion. If the story was untrue, then who might these men be? Secret agents or trained Fifth Columnists, arriving in advance of the troops to pass information back and spread alarm and confusion once the guns opened fire? In either case the matter was too big for him to handle. He picked up the telephone.

The news passed quickly to the highest authorities. Soon the Home Secretary, the Cabinet and the Prime Minister himself, Mr. Winston Churchill, had heard the facts. From the top came the orders. The fullest inquiries were to be made into the state of the country's defenses and in particular how they could permit these men who spoke no English to land at will and wander on their way to London without once being noticed or questioned. A peremptory order went out to M.I.5 demanding that the three men should be most thoroughly investigated.

This is the point where I entered the story.

2

By this time the three men had been transferred from Cannon Row Police Station to the Royal Victoria Patriotic School in Trinity Road, Clapham. No doubt the police inspector breathed a sigh of relief to see the back of his odd charges, leaving him free to deal with the more familiar job of looking after the straightforward criminals of London.

Before starting my interrogation, I closely studied the three men. They were an ill-assorted crew. The first, whom I suspected to be the weakest in personality, was no more than a boy in his teens. He had soft, downy cheeks and downcast eyes and kept on biting his lip as though to restrain the tears that were not far from the surface. The second was of different caliber, a stocky, square-shouldered man with the build of a wrestler. He was swarthy and physically strong but mentally not very alert. His eyes

68

flickered continually around the room, sliding restlessly across every object and never stopping in their quest. I judged him to be a man of considerable low cunning but without much initiative.

The third man was obviously the ringleader. Having myself hunted big game and also having been the owner of a private zoo in what seemed the far-off days of peace, at the first sight of him I thought of the jungle beasts I had known well. His movements were supple and easy and he stood before me poised and menacing in his muscular control. His face was scarred with knife scars and those other jagged semicircular scars which result from the edges of a broken bottle that has been thrust against a man's face and then viciously twisted. One such scar lifted his upper lip in a perpetual grimace. There were bald patches on his scalp and these too were the work of the knife or the broken bottle. As he stood there, watching me coolly, his personality dominated the trio. The others were manifestly in fear of him. They were far more impressed by a glance from him than they were by the power of officialdom as represented by me. Yes, Monsieur Magis, which was the name he had given to the police inspector, was the man to watch. He told me in brief the story of their escape from France and their landing on the northeast coast, which the other two listened to impassively. There would be no opportunity of getting the others to speak for themselves while in the presence of the ringleader, so I decided to break off the joint interview and interrogate them individually.

69

3

First of all I sent for the "baby" of the trio, the soft-faced young man who had hardly opened his mouth up to this point. He was patently nervous when he entered the room so that I tried to reassure him by chatting about trivialities while he sat down. He continued to twist his fingers and glance over his shoulder as though he were expecting the formidable Monsieur Magis to pounce on him, but gradually he became less restless.

"Now then," I said. We were speaking French, the only language he seemed to know. "This is really a formality but I have to ask you various questions—for the record. We are most impressed with your gallant and successful effort at escaping and we should like to know more details. For instance, what time of the day did you land? Morning, afternoon, night?"

"I think it was about two in the afternoon, sir."

"Good. Now what kind of boat did you—er, borrow. A sailing boat? Or was it a rowing boat? Or perhaps you were lucky enough to find a motor boat?"

"It was a sailing boat, sir. But it had oars which we could use if the wind dropped."

"I see. Now what about the spot where you landed? Was it a rocky place or was the beach sandy?"

"It was sandy, sir. Sort of sloping."

"Well, that made things easier, didn't it? No risk of smashing the boat on the rocks. By the way, what was the color of the boat?"

He hesitated and then said, "Gray, sir."

70

"That's all I wanted to know. Nothing very frightening in that, was there?"

"No, sir." He gave me a shy smile and left the room. I sat thinking for a moment and then sent for the stocky strong man with the shifting eyes.

4

The next interview followed the same lines. After putting my visitor at his ease and apologizing for having to ask him a few questions, I said casually, "Well, old chap, do you remember what time the three of you landed?"

He went through the motions of remembering, jaw clasped in one massive hand and a scowl of concentration on his far from handsome features. Then the evasive memory returned and his face lit up. "It would be—let me see—about nine o'clock in the morning, sir. Judging by the sun, that is. The only watch we had was broken."

"Thank you. Now how about that petrol for the engine? This is rather important. If you've found out a new way of tricking the Gestapo, it may be valuable for helping other refugees to escape. You see the point? So give me the details, will you?"

"Yes, of course, sir. Glad to help. As it turned out, it was easy. This friend of mine in Brittany, he's a fisherman. He'd buried a few cans of petrol in his garden. He let us dig them up in the night."

"H-m, very clever. Now what about the coast you landed on? Anything peculiar about it? Were there cliffs or rocks or was it an ordinary beach?"

71

"Well, not exactly a beach, sir. There were sand dunes dotted about. The shore line was rather steep and we had to climb up it, holding onto trees and bushes. They looked like pine trees."

"What happened to the boat?"

"Oh, we had to let it go. No hope of beaching it, sir."

"Well, that's all the questioning. Oh, by the way, what did you say the color of the boat was?"

"Brown, sir."

I thanked him with a nod and a smile and he swaggered out of the room. I had given orders for the three of them to be segregated so there was no risk that they would compare notes.

5

"Come in, Monsieur Magis," I said. "Sit down and make yourself at home."

He took me at my word, lolled back, swung one knee across the other and looked around with an air of proprietorship.

"I have to ask you a few questions," I said. "A pure formality, of course, but you know what officials are like. Always filling up forms and reports and passing them to and fro."

Magis nodded. He knew about officials.

"Well now, what time was it you landed in England? I'll have to put that in my report, you see."

"Naturally," said Magis. He tapped one of the many scars on his cheek with a forefinger. "It must have been

72

about six o'clock in the late afternoon." He paused and then nodded. "Yes, that's about it. Six o'clock, within half an hour either way."

"Thank you. Now I believe you landed on a nasty part of the coast, all rocks and so forth. Must have been rather tricky, wasn't it? Any trouble getting ashore?"

"It wasn't pleasant. At one time I thought it was going to be hopeless. It looked as though the boat would be smashed on the rocks but . . ."

"But then you spotted that creek?"

A momentary look of surprise flashed over Magis's face.

"Yes, we did. Just our luck. The sea was pretty smooth just there and somehow we managed to steer the boat into it. We scrambled ashore as best we could but the boat—" he shrugged his shoulders.

"Don't worry about the boat. There are plenty more of them. Show me your hands, please?"

Magis looked surprised. "My hands, what do you mean?" But he held his hands, palms upward, for my inspection.

I shook my head. "I don't understand it at all. Your two friends confirm that the boat had no sail and no motor, just a couple of oars. There you were, rowing away for four days and four nights, but there's not a single blister on either of your hands. I just don't understand it."

Magis thought fast. "Well, it may seem odd to you, sir, but there's an easy explanation. Feel my hands. They're very hard, you know. I don't blister easily. Besides, surely you don't think I did all the rowing? We took it in turns, one after the other, and nobody rowed long enough to get

73

tired out. And another thing. Most of the time we didn't row at all. Just drifted with the current for hours on end. Do you follow now, sir?

I shrugged my shoulders. "That may be the right explantation. In any case, it's not important. But what I do fail to see is why you didn't change the color of your boat. Weren't you worried that the Germans would spot you from miles away? That bright red boat must have stuck out like a sore thumb."

"Yes," admitted Monsieur Magis. "It certainly was a risk. But we had to take it. There was no time to waste in painting the boat. Besides, where would we have got all that paint from at short notice?"

"Don't ask me," I answered. "I was never much of a painter."

"Any other questions, sir? I'm always pleased to be at your service."

"Thank you, Magis. I appreciate that. But that's all for now. Let's have your two friends along. I'd like a little chat with you all together."

A few minutes later the other two men arrived under guard. I told them to sit down and stared at them each in turn. The "baby" studied the floor and did not dare look up. The strong man looked everywhere except into my eyes. Only Magis, the ringleader, returned my stare as coolly as could be.

"Well," I said at last, "I'm looking at three liars. Three very foolish, stupid liars. Why, even little boys playing truant from school make sure that the details of their ex-

74

cuses agree. Yet you big men, so clever and tough, make the most childish mistakes. You," pointing to the youngest, "say you landed in England at two in the afternoon. But when it comes to your turn," looking at the shifty-eyed man, "the time has mysteriously changed to nine in the morning. Whereas you, Magis, arrived at six o'clock in the evening. The same boat but it arrived at three different times. This wonderful boat had another magical property— it could change its color like a chameleon. At one time it was gray, then it became brown and when I suggested that it was bright red you, Magis, did not correct me. Even more miraculous, the boat could change its method of propulsion at will. It started life as a sailing boat but somewhere on the high seas it acquired a petrol engine—just so that you could use the petrol so thoughtfully dug up from the garden of your Breton fisher friend. Yet you spend the trip rowing hard, Magis, although there is not a trace of a blister on your hands. Even if one could swallow those stupid and outstanding lies, the very seashore changed as each one of you approached it. At one moment it was sandy and sloping. Before long dunes and pine trees sprang up from nowhere and when it comes to your turn, Magis, rocks suddenly emerged. What kind of a fool do you take me for, gentlemen?"

There was no answer. They sat there stolidly.

"There is only one obvious explanation," I went on. "There never was a boat or a seashore. However you arrived in England, of one thing I am certain. You did not

75

arrive in the way you have so stupidly described. Now I want the truth. How did you get here?"

There was complete silence. I looked from one to the other but they avoided my eyes. Then Magis broke in and had the temerity to say that his story was correct in every detail. He refused to admit that there were flaws in it. What he said was the truth, the whole truth and nothing but the truth. I could take it or leave it. It didn't matter to him.

"That's where you make a big mistake, my friend," I replied. "It does matter to you—very much. In spite of your assertions, your stories simply don't stand up. If you are honest men, genuine refugees, why should you tell me these trumped-up tales? The implication is that you are not genuine. If you are not genuine, why have you come here? The answer is simple—you are three spies. Do you know what we do to spies that are caught? Early one morning, after they have had a good breakfast, if they can manage to swallow it down, we take them for a short walk to the scaffold, put a rope around their necks—and hang them."

I stared at them again, at their faces and their necks. No one said a word. The other two glanced furtively at Magis and once the "baby" licked his lips but no one broke the silence. They were obviously still more scared of Magis than they were of the prospect of being hanged as spies. But time and the opportunity to think things over might change their perspective. I nodded to the guards to take them away.

6

It is said of boxers that the bigger they are the harder they fall. It has often been my experience in interrogations that the tougher a man appears to be the quicker he tends to crack under pressure. The outer shell of the supposedly tough man is often more brittle than the soft pliancy of the apparent weakling. I decided, therefore, to concentrate my efforts on Monsieur Magis. I ordered him to be removed from the Royal Victoria Patriotic School to a more severely disciplined establishment on purely military lines which was situated in Chelsea. There he was interrogated again and again. The damning evidence of the three conflicting accounts of their arrival was dinned into him by constant repetition. Continually he was warned of the fate that befell spies caught in wartime. But he did not turn a hair of his scarred head. As often as he was questioned he repeated that he had told the truth and only the truth. How could he help it if no one believed him? That was our hypercritical fault, not his. As for the fact that his two friends had told stories which varied from his a little, that was easily explained. They were a pair of fools anyway, without an abundance of brains between them. Surely we could see that? They had memories like sieves and, being anxious to help, had made up what they couldn't really remember. Anyone could set a trap for fools like that to fall into. Why not interrogate them again, now that they had had time in which to sort their ideas out? We would find that their memories had improved by now.

I decided to take Magis at his word. I personally interro-

77

gated the other two again. I might have saved myself the trouble. They confirmed the details of Magis's story at every point. Yes, they had both been wrong in their versions. They had been tired and suffering from nervous exhaustion, after their arduous journey. Now they had had time to reflect, they realized that Magis was entirely right and that they had been wrong. Yes, of course, the boat had been red and the coast rocky. No, certainly it had never possessed a sail or a petrol engine. And so on.

All I gained from these interviews was the further proof that both of them were mortally afraid of Magis, so afraid that they would risk the condemned cell to support his fantastic story. But I was all the more positive that these two men were not spies. In my thirty years of experience in counterespionage I had met many spies but none quite like this pair. For one thing they lacked either the intelligence or the shrewdness of the spy. The Germans might make mistakes but they were thoroughgoing professionals at their trade. At such a crucial stage of the war, they would not toss a pair of rank amateurs into the country they hoped to invade. The first thing that professional spies would do would be to agree on the details of their story and thereafter stick to what they had agreed. Magis might possibly be a professional spy but I would stake my reputation that his two companions were not. Yet how came it that these three who could not speak a word of English should have teamed up together? And for what purpose?

Time was growing short and the highest authorities were impatiently pressing for results. So far I had tried all the conventional methods and in this unconventional situation they had failed hopelessly. I was convinced that Magis was the ringleader and that I was right to concentrate my efforts on him. He was going to be my "canary," I was sure, but how could he be made to sing?

An unconventional idea struck me. It seemed the only way of making him talk, short of physical torture which, even if it had not been completely repugnant to me, would never have been allowed. But I had to get the co-operation of the other officers in the establishment to put my idea into effect. The intelligence officer was all for novelty. When I spoke to him, he soon became enthusiastic and, better still, infected the others, even the commanding officer, who rather grudgingly allowed me to go ahead.

The first step was to transfer Magis to a darkened cell where he spent a day and a night in solitary confinement. Next morning he was marched under escort into a large room. He was halted in front of a table covered with green baize. Behind the table sat the officers of the establishment, each in full service dress, buttons highly polished, leather Sam Browne belts glistening and peaked caps on their heads. On the table in front of each one lay his Army revolver. As the official presiding over the "court-martial" I sat at the center of the long table.

It was an impressive sight, particularly for a man who had just spent twenty-four hours in the darkness with only his thoughts for company. As Magis stood there between the two guards with their bayonets fixed, he blinked once or twice. There was a minute or two of absolute silence to

79

allow him time to realize the solemnity of the occasion. Already his air of cocky superiority was slipping.

I spoke to him in French. "Prisoner at the bar, do you know where you have spent the last twenty-four hours?"

"Yes, sir. In a dark cell."

"Do you know what kind of cell it is?"

"N-no, sir." He looked puzzled, perturbed.

"It is the condemned cell. Men who enter it have reached the next to last stage in their mortal journey."

I paused and there was silence in the room except for the prisoner's breathing. He was not yet panting but his breath came quicker than was normal. I went on.

"Prisoner at the bar, you were arrested in London and have been given every opportunity of telling the military authorities the truth about yourself. Yet you have persisted in telling a cock-and-bull story which, by the evidence of your own comrades, is false in every detail. In spite of the damning evidence against you, you still claim that your story is true. The facts are against you, prisoner at the bar. There is only one possible explanation for your continued lying. You have been sent here by the enemy as a spy or a Fifth Columnist. In wartime that is an offense punishable with death!

"You are now appearing before a court-martial which has assembled for the express purpose of trying you. There is only one verdict the court can reach. That is 'Guilty.' And there is only one sentence that can be passed—'Death by hanging.'

"In spite of your attitude and your brazen lying, we are

80

prepared to give you one last chance." I took out my watch and placed it on the green baize table in front of me. "You will have exactly two minutes in which to decide whether you will tell us the truth at last or whether you will go to the gallows with a lie on your lips. Think it over carefully. This is your last chance. Two minutes from now your time will be up."

There was no sound in the room but the precise metallic ticking of the watch. One by one the seconds were bringing Magis nearer his fate. He stared at the floor, breathing silently, almost as though he were deliberately holding his breath. The noises of London at work, the humming of traffic and the braying of a distant, impatient motor horn filtered into the room, letting normality into this bizarre situation. The second hand of the watch had completed one cycle. Still Magis stood there, head bowed, but giving no indication of losing his nerve. One of the escort shuffled his feet and in the hushed atmosphere the sound was like a pistol shot.

The two minutes were up. I put my watch away and stared at Magis. "Prisoner at the bar, what have you to say?"

He looked me straight in the eye. "Nothing."

"That is your final answer?"

"Yes."

I rose to my feet slowly. "You have brought your own death on yourself. I shall now pronounce sentence." Covering my head with a piece of black silk, I spoke the words that every man condemned to death hears in an English

81

court of law. "The sentence of the court upon you is that you be taken from this place to a lawful prison and thence to a place of execution; that you there suffer death by hanging and that your body be afterward buried in the precincts of the prison in which you have been confined before your execution . . . and may the Lord have mercy on your soul."

I sat down and gazed at the prisoner. I waited for a moment, expecting him to break and babble out the truth. But he did not stir. He just stared at the floor. As I nodded to the two guards to march him away, the suspicion seized me that he had seen through the impressive charade we had acted for his benefit. The door had hardly closed behind him and the sound of footsteps could still be heard in the corridor outside, when there was the hiss of escaping breath from both sides of me. The other officers shifted in their chairs and the tension relaxed.

But an embarrassed silence prevailed. Everyone gazed at me. At last the commanding officer, clearing his throat, muttered what was in the minds of all. "Well, where do we go from here?"

Normally I can control my emotions with some success but on this occasion I felt the hot flush of confusion creeping up my neck into my cheeks. My supposedly brilliant and unconventional idea had been a complete failure. Far from being cowed, the prisoner had shrugged his way through it without giving himself away. He had had the grace not to laugh out loud at our play-acting but that was the only slight satisfaction to be salvaged out of the wreck

82

of my hopes. We had all been made fools of, and none worse than I, the originator of this stupid idea. I gathered my wits and in my mortification managed to reply: "Gentlemen, can we wait for a moment? There is just a chance that the prisoner may have second thoughts and . . ." My voice trailed away and I could feel the skeptical glances on my averted face.

Just then there was a knock on the door. It opened and one of the sentries who had escorted Magis entered. "Sir," he said, saluting, "the prisoner would like to know if he can speak to you."

I swallowed the smile that was almost on my lips and, trying to keep the "I-told-you-so" tone out of my voice, answered, "All right, march him in."

Magis was marched in.

"What do you want?" I asked sharply.

The perpetual half smile, formed by the scar tissue on his puckered upper lip, broadened as he sprang another surprise in this day of surprises. "Well, sir, I'd better come clean. . . ."

I absorbed the shock by jerking back. Not only had he spoken in English, a language he supposedly did not know, but the accent and the idiom were obviously transatlantic.

"Yes," I replied, "you had better come clean. You're a Canadian, aren't you?"

"Yes, sir, French-Canadian."

So one problem was solved. Magis and his two comrades were deserters from the Canadian Forces stationed in England. But this was not the moment to draw a neat line

83

across the bottom of the page and file yet another completed dossier. A bigger and more complicated problem was just beginning.

7

Before Magis had time to regain his nerve, I gave him another long bout of questioning. There were two points in particular that I wanted to establish. One was the reason which had made him persist in his unlikely story up to the stage where he was "condemned to death." The other was what had happened to his uniform and his Army pay book, the soldier's normal means of identifying himself. Magis and his two friends had had to look after themselves from the time they deserted to the day they were arrested. How had they done so and how did they acquire the money they had spent?

The answer to the first problem was reasonable. Magis had already been a deserter on eight separate occasions. He had been warned the last time that another similar offense would earn him at least two years of imprisonment in the "Glasshouse" at Aldershot. (Rightly or wrongly, the "Glasshouse" was the military prison more feared than any other by soldiers. Potential inmates spoke of it in hushed tones.) Rather than risk a two-year spell there Magis was prepared to bluff things out up to the point where he seemed likely to suffer a worse fate.

As for the pay book and the uniform, the answer to the first was that he had burned it on breaking camp and to the second that he had met a man in Soho who was pre-

84

pared to give him a civilian suit in good condition and a sum of money as well in exchange for his worn battledress. He did not know the fairy godmother's name or why he should have been so quixotic.

But a sinister suspicion was already forming in my mind. I did not believe that tale about burning the Army pay book. A deserter on the run might conceivably throw it away, although he would be hard put to establish his identity without it, if he were stopped and questioned. Burning it was too thorough a means of destroying something that was not sufficiently incriminating to warrant destruction. It was more likely that Magis and his friends had sold their pay books along with their uniforms. And the only client for this kind of transaction would not be a secondhand clothes dealer but, it seemed probable to me, the organizer of a Fifth Column. At any day Hitler might launch his long-awaited invasion against England. The technique had already been demonstrated in France and Belgium and Holland. After the Stuka dive bombers had swooped, confusion and panic would break out. Refugees would cram the roads and immobilize military traffic. Fifth Columnists would be used to swell the panic and confusion by spreading false rumors and by further dislocating military traffic. In the heat of the moment two or three men in uniform could stand at a crossroads and divert convoys down the wrong turnings. Or they could persuade or order civilians to vacate their homes and thus add to the confusion. The bulk of the Canadian troops was stationed in southeast England, the most likely invasion area. Was this the reason,

I wondered, why Canadian-type battledresses were in demand? And who was the buyer?

I interrogated the other two deserters again but, although they now realized from the details I knew that Magis had confessed, they could not add much to his story. He had so obviously been the ringleader that they followed him blindly. They did, however, confirm that the pay books had been handed over with the uniforms and not burned. Having by this stage exhausted their slight usefulness I arranged for them to be handed over for trial by their own authorities and at the same time asked permission for Magis to be detained by M.I.5 pending further investigations. The Canadian military authorities agreed at once. The Home Office was also given the explanation of the so-called "landings," which set many minds at rest.

In my opinion, however, this second problem was even more important. If a Fifth Column organization were at work, it had to be suppressed at once. But to try to do so was outside my normal sphere and beyond my powers of authority. I visited Scotland Yard and there had an interview with a superintendent of the Special Branch. He was at first inclined to be suspicious of the "amateurs" of M.I.5 trespassing on his territory and it touched his professional pride to be told that things might be going on in Soho, the nerve center of London's crime, of which he was totally unaware. We had a long discussion and this very able officer soon thawed out. In the end I left him with the generous assurance that the Special Branch could put at my disposal two police cars and a hand-picked squad for the next three weeks. The object—night operations in Soho.

8

There followed a further series of interrogations between Magis and myself. He cheerfully agreed that he had told yet another lie in pretending to have burned his pay book when I confronted him with the evidence of his two friends. Gradually he became more malleable and, knowing that he might get a reduction of the military conviction that was coming to him if he co-operated with us, he really did do his best to help. But, as he pointed out, he had only met the go-between, who had offered to buy the uniforms, once or twice. The streets were blacked out and the Soho pubs were crowded with a strange, shifting population. Was it any wonder, he claimed, that he could not describe the go-between with any accuracy?

Strangely enough, I grew to like Magis who, in spite of his desperado's appearance and his ability to lie and cheat with the utmost coolness, had a sense of humor that appealed to me. I came to enjoy our conversations, although both of us began to realize that they were not advancing matters one step. It seemed that Magis's usefulness had become exhausted and as the days went by without results I knew that I should have to look elsewhere before long.

Magis must have suspected my intentions and decided that if he could not help me he might at least put on some entertainment. One day as we began yet another interview he put his hand in his pocket and produced an old razor

87

blade. Before I could stop him he calmly placed it in his mouth, chewed away with complete unconcern and then swallowed it, opening his mouth triumphantly to show that there was no deception. As an encore he produced a chunk of broken glass, the fragment of a beer bottle, from the same pocket and coolly crunched it into powder and then swallowed it. I had heard of glass and razor-blade eaters before but had never seen one at such close quarters. Every second I expected to see a trickle of blood from his lips but he chewed and swallowed with the utmost unconcern and apparent enjoyment.

"What the devil's the meaning of this farce?" I demanded. Magis looked hurt. "I was only giving a performance," he said. "That's the way I earn my living."

"Your living?" I echoed. "You eat glass for a living?"

"Sure. There's hardly a fun fair in Canada or the States that hasn't seen me. The folks all roll up when I go into my routine. That's how we made some dough here in London after we broke out."

I chuckled. All at once I began to see how Magis might be of further use. Magis—the French abbreviation for "conjurer." I ought perhaps to have wondered before how he earned his strange name.

The plan was a simple one. Magis, with myself in attendance, would wander through the Soho pubs at night, putting on his act if and when necessary. A squad of plain-clothes policemen would follow us at a discreet distance since many of them would be recognized and we did not want their presence to be linked with ours. Sooner or later we ought to bump into Magis's "friend."

I propounded the plan to Magis and asked, "Well, are you game?"

"Sure, I'm game. Anything to get a breath of fresh air away from this dump. Say, who pays for the drinks?"

"His Majesty's Government. But don't think this is a spree. It's strictly business. And one word of advice. Don't try any funny business. One false move and you'll end up by qualifying as the oldest inhabitant of the Glasshouse. Do you get that?"

Magis got it.

9

The first night we drew a complete blank. No sooner had we reached Soho than the air-raid sirens began to wail. A few minutes later we could hear the irregular droning of German bombers overhead and then searchlights probed the black sky. Soon the barking of ack-ack guns mingled with the screeching and thudding of bombs; shrapnel from the exploding shells pattered on the streets like steel raindrops. The narrow streets of Soho were deserted, as everyone, criminals and honest men alike, took to the air-raid shelters. After several hours of fruitless searching we decided to call off the hunt for that night.

The second evening we were again confronted with an air raid almost as soon as we reached the hunting ground but fortunately it did not last long. Groping through the black-out, we slipped into one pub after another, our eyes smarting from the almost palpable fug of stale air and tobacco smoke that hit us as we opened the door and plucked aside the heavy black-out curtains that usually hung over the entrance. Magis and I would push our way toward some vantage point near the bar and order a half pint of that tepid beverage known to the English as beer. A babel of accents and languages would be deafening us on all sides. Cautiously Magis would look over the rim of his glass and see if he could spot his "friend" among the men of different shapes, sizes and colors that crowded the room. He would invariably give a slight shake of his head and after we had spent a few more minutes in idle conversation we would push our way toward the door and grope through the blacked-out streets for the next pub. We would give the plain-clothes man who was trailing us time to catch up and then the same routine would take place.

The hour was late, our success was nil and I was rapidly losing my patience. Indigestion through too many half pints of warm and watery beer was attacking me and my head ached with the stuffy atmosphere of frowsty pubs. I was beginning to wonder whether this bright idea had not rapidly developed into a wild-goose chase. The prospect of clean sheets and a soft pillow grew more alluring every moment. Just as I was thinking of calling off the fruitless hunt, we had a stroke of luck. Magis and I were in a pub in Charlotte Street. The pub was less full than others we had visited and as we strolled toward the bar I happened to intercept a swift exchange of glances between Magis and a swarthy, youngish man who was leaning against the bar. That was all. The young man casually emptied his glass and without another look in Magis's direction unobtrusively moved toward the door. I nodded to a plain-clothes detective who had followed us in and he slipped out after the swarthy man. I pulled Magis on one side.

"Well, he was your man. Right?"

Magis nodded.

"Why the hell didn't you say so? Or go up and talk to him? Are you trying to double-cross me?"

For almost the first time in our acquaintance Magis looked confused. He muttered something about "squealing" and then I realized how strongly the code of the underworld and of its fringe on which men like himself moved had gripped him. The best of intentions had melted when he was confronted face to face with the man he had set out to betray.

10

But that chance encounter was not in vain. The detective returned much later that night with a great deal of information. The go-between turned out to be a tailor's apprentice who was not a British subject but of French origin. He had no criminal record and there was not the slightest suspicion that he had ever been anything but a most circumspect citizen. It was too big a coincidence, however, that we were hunting for missing uniforms and that he earned his living by sewing and cutting clothes. He was arrested and cross-examined. He broke down and gave us the name and address of the next link in the chain.

This next man called himself a physical culture instruc-

91

tor and, on being pressed, gave us instructions which, though neither physical nor cultural, proved to be invaluable. He gave us an address in Romilly Street, Soho, and as he spoke the detectives who knew the district well nodded significantly. The occupant of this address was apparently known as "The Terror of Soho," a criminal with over thirty convictions ranging from dope peddling to robbery with violence. Now at last we were getting somewhere.

That night we arrived at the door of the third-floor flat in that house in Romilly Street. We rang the bell. Nobody answered. We rapped on the door with our knuckles. Still no answer. We tried the door. It was locked.

"Well, there's only one thing for it," I said. "Let's go."

Opening a locked door by force is child's play to burly, experienced policemen. In a few seconds the sustained pressure of shoulders, backs and feet took the door off its hinges and we rushed in. All was silent and deserted in the flat until we reached the bedroom. A woman lay asleep in a big double bed. From her stertorous breathing it was obvious that she was heavily drugged and would be senseless for many hours to come.

One of the plain-clothes men muttered, "I've seen her before. She's The Terror's mistress. A well-known drug addict."

The pillow beside her head was dented. Slipping a hand into the side of the bed away from her inert form, I could feel a patch that was still warm. Someone, presumably The Terror, had been sharing the bed with her up to a few

92

minutes ago. We tiptoed up to the attic, which was filthy—and empty. There was only one more place to try—the roof.

And there we found The Terror, huddled behind a chimney. Shivering in his thin pajamas, he was an abject sight as he meekly surrendered to the first challenge. The Terror of Soho was, like many of his breed, more terrified than terrorizing when the Law caught up with him.

While he was dressing we searched his flat. We discovered a large quantity of cocaine and stocks of indecent literature but not a sign of uniforms and Army pay books. But when The Terror was safely back in my office and was confronted with the warning that the goods found in his flat would be enough to put him behind the bars for many years if he failed to co-operate with us, he broke down completely. Not for him the code of the underworld to which Magis had subscribed the night before. As the vital information came tumbling out, I realized with contempt that this so-called "big shot" of crime would cheerfully betray his own mother to save his skin. The Terror told who the ringleaders were in this industry of procuring uniforms, where they could be found and where their business premises were. I telephoned the information to Scotland Yard and before daylight all the leaders were safely in the hands of the police. The flourishing industry had gone abruptly into involuntary liquidation.

The most comforting piece of information given by The Terror related to the purpose of this amazing industry. There was no organized Fifth Column work behind it. I rapidly learned that the average Soho criminal thought exclusively in terms of personal gain or personal safety. He lacked both the fanaticism and the inverted patriotism that would enable him to betray his (usually adopted) country to the enemy. The uniforms were required for a subtle and impudent trick. The teeming streets of Soho, which is almost like a separate village inside the largest city in the world, were often entered by civilian policemen but rarely, if ever, by military policemen. To avoid conscription into the forces men of military age were prepared to pay large sums of money to buy a uniform and papers belonging to someone else. Equipped with these, they could "enter" the Army without the formality of taking the oath of allegiance, of medical examination and drilling on the barrack square. The risk of being found out was comparatively small. The police would be looking for deserters *out of* uniform and draft dodgers, not the often bemedaled "heroes" in uniform who would apparently be enjoying a well-earned leave.

Once the gang who had organized the buying and selling of uniforms and pay books was rounded up, the Special Branch of Scotland Yard turned its activities to arresting the many hundreds of deserters out of uniform and the "dodgers" in uniform. With the collaboration of the Military Police, the hunt went on for several months and was largely successful.

I never saw Magis again after he had been handed over to the Canadian military authorities. If he was able to get into action after serving his sentence, I have no doubt that he distinguished himself. He was a brave, resourceful man,

94

not an ornament to soldiering under peacetime conditions but a good comrade to have beside one if there was fighting to be done. As for The Terror who talked, he also was of considerable future help to me but not in a way that demanded courage. Having acquired a taste for talking, he became a paid informer and occasionally gave me useful tips. The path of virtue proved rather too narrow for him in the end. When I last heard of him, he was serving yet another term of four years' hard labor for robbery with violence.

CHAPTER VI

The Spy-catcher Helps the Spies

IN THE First World War healthy-looking young men not in uniform ran the risk of being stopped by a woman and handed a white feather. The implication of this act was obvious. Why were they not doing their bit in the fighting line? Were they afraid to enlist? Very often men home on leave who had changed out of uniform or men who looked fit enough but had some serious defect which was not visible to the naked eye, a weak heart perhaps, suffered this public humiliation.

Fortunately the barbarous custom was not in evidence much in the Second World War. There was not the same feeling that a man who was not in uniform was a skulking coward. Everyone, soldier or civilian, was in the war and when air raids or flying bombs arrived, each stood an equal chance of dying suddenly as a war casualty. In fact, ironically enough, many a civilian in London and the other big towns was in greater danger of death than were soldiers in uniform stationed in the Middle East and elsewhere. Nevertheless, custom dies hard and mothers whose sons might have been killed in the services or who were running the daily risk of being killed would look askance at the hefty young men who seemed to live in luxury in London's

96

West End, without doing a hand's turn for the war effort. There were indeed some draft dodgers and deserters, but on the whole comparatively few. The young men who lived in apparent idleness in luxury flats and who disappeared mysteriously, sometimes never to return, were not what would be called in postwar slang "spivs" but—secret agents.

I have the utmost admiration for such men. Indeed any secret agent, whether he is acting for or against one's own country, deserves admiration for his courage alone. It is one thing to be brave in company but a different matter to be brave on one's own when every passer-by or acquaintance is a potential betrayer, when vigilance must be exercised during every waking hour and even subconsciously in sleep, lest the secret agent should talk in his sleep in his native tongue and give himself away. No one who has not been "on the run" or lived a long time with secret agents can realize the strain of being constantly on guard, never knowing whether the man approaching from behind is going to pat one on the back out of friendship or clap a heavy hand on one's shoulder in the act of arrest.

These secret agents in the service of the British Government, whose life of apparent luxury in the West End of London brought withering glances from the uninitiated, had to be young and in perfect health. Their usual method of reaching their objective was by parachute; after the age of forty a man's muscles get too stiff for a parachute drop on a dark night when the ground below may be rough and he may suffer an unpleasant tumble. Many of the secret

97

agents were foreigners who would drop out of the sky onto their native soil, sometimes near their own home towns. Several of them had their faces changed by plastic surgery so that they would not be recognized by friends and relations. The others were Englishmen who knew the Continent and one of the different languages so well that they could pass as natives.

For months before they were ready for operations such men went through a most rigorous course of training in parachuting and learning the use of explosives for sabotage work. They were kept at a spy school in the depths of the country and their curriculum included the art of disguise, the various methods of killing a man silently, the use of all hand weapons, wireless operating, knowledge of secret inks, photography and revision as to physical details of the locality they would be visiting. The standard of the course, both physically and mentally, was of a high order and only pupils who passed the various tests were allowed to proceed. The discipline was Spartan; the potential agents were never encouraged to take one drink too many or to have girl friends. Romance is nearly always fatal to the spy, whose emotions must be under control.

Then these young men, trained to a pitch of mental and physical excellence, were dispatched on their dangerous tasks. And yet in spite of all their careful training the mortality rate among them was alarmingly high. In one case, the notorious "England Spiel," many courageous young Dutch agents were caught and examined by the Gestapo because, in spite of all precautions taken, a traitor had

98

managed to infiltrate into their ranks. But on other occasions news gradually leaked out that the agents were being caught through their own blunders. This was a most distressing situation. Not only did it mean that the months of careful preparation were being wasted and that valuable information about our own methods was falling into enemy hands but it also made our authorities wonder whether the hazards were not too great to be undertaken. It is one thing to ask a brave man to take a ten-to-one risk. He has a chance of coming through. But when the odds are a hundred to one or perhaps a hundred to nil no one would dare to ask a brave, intelligent man, whose qualities could be of immense use to his country, to commit virtual suicide.

At this point someone in authority realized that Counter-Intelligence officers, who were already gaining firsthand experience at catching secret agents, might be used to test our own secret agents before they set off on their hazardous journeys. If a secret agent could pass the most searching tests devised by experts at spy-catching he would have greater confidence in his ability to outwit the Gestapo at a later date. If he broke down under the test that his own people put him through, his failure instead of proving fatal might teach him how to avoid repeating his mistakes. After this sensible decision had been reached, I was invited to examine the next batch of secret agents before they left England. I was asked to give them the most rigorous examination I could think of and, without actually inflicting physical torture on any of them, to adapt my methods as nearly as possible to those practiced by the Gestapo.

A few days later, three young men reported to my office. They were good physical specimens, obviously trained to the last hair. Their faces glowed and their eyes shone with perfect health and fitness. They were three fine young men, alert and intelligent.

I turned to the official who stood there, obviously full of pride and confidence in his protégés. "When do they leave?" I asked.

"The day after tomorrow," he replied.

"Just as they are?"

"Yes, just as they are now."

I looked again at the three young men. Their clothes were neat and unobtrusive, neither new nor shabby. They looked indeed like the three young Belgian businessmen they were intended to resemble. I walked over to the nearest, put my hand inside the top of his waistcoat and pulled out his tie. I turned it over. The shop label sewn on the reverse proclaimed: "Selfridges, Oxford Street, London, W.1."

"Take them away," I said to the official who now looked crestfallen. "After that there is no point in my asking them questions."

With my room to myself again, I slumped in a chair and lit a cigarette. No wonder, I thought, that brave men are going daily to their death if that is the kind of silly slip which is being permitted. It seemed fantastic that no pains were being spared to bring these young agents to the highest pitch of physical and mental training and yet the most obvious and glaring precautions were being omitted. I

100

shook my head sadly at the time, money and valuable human lives that must have been wasted already.

Six days later I was asked to examine another young man who was soon to be dropped by parachute in Belgium. This time one lesson had been learned. There was not a stitch of English clothing to betray him.

I asked him to tell me the "cover story" which he might have to tell the Gestapo to explain his previous movements and his reasons for being wherever he happened to be found. This is the story he told me. When the Germans had taken Belgium, he had fled to the South of France. Arriving at Nice, he had eventually found a job in a flower plantation. He had worked there as a laborer for eight months but when he heard that conditions in Belgium were better under the Nazis than had been expected, he decided to return to Brussels. Figuratively speaking, here he was.

"What did you say your job was on this flower plantation?" I asked him in Flemish.

"Laboring, sir."

"Show me your hands." He held them out for my inspection. The finger tips were soft; there were no ridges of hard skin across the palms; the fingernails were well tended and none of them was cracked or discolored. No man alive could have worked for eight months as a laborer in a flower plantation and retained the hands of an office worker.

I sighed, partly out of pity and partly through exasperation. "Well then," I said, "tell me some more about this flower plantation. What flowers did you grow?"

101

"Oh, roses and [a pause] carnations." He fell silent.

"Fuchsias?" I prompted.

"No, not fuchsias."

"Primulas?"

"Oh yes, we grew primulas."

"So you grew primulas? On the Mediterranean coast! My dear boy, you are supposed to be something of an expert on flowers. Remember? You worked for eight months in a plantation. Do you really know anything at all about flowers, I wonder? Go back to your instructors and tell them that you are wasting my time and unnecessarily risking your own life."

After this experience, I introduced "the story inside a story" technique, which has already been stated in the Appendix to Chapter II, to the instructors at the secret agents' school. Human nature is such that we are always more likely to believe a story that discredits the teller than a story that shows him to advantage. The Gestapo examiners in particular, who from the very nature of their job would be prone to see the worst in all men, would be far more ready to accept a confession of human weakness. This young man with his story of working at a flower plantation should, for example, have been equipped with "a story inside a story." Having been confronted with the improbability of his original story and no doubt tortured into the bargain by the Gestapo, he should then appear to break down at the earliest likely moment and gasp out, "For God's sake stop. I'll tell you the truth. I can't stand any more. I didn't spend eight months in Nice—and I never

102

saw a flower plantation. I was only there a few days. I hadn't a sou so I started begging. There was one woman, she was at least fifty, an awful old hag with hair dyed a bright red. She took a fancy to me and took me home with her. I couldn't stand her after a couple of days. She meant well but did she want her money's worth! You're men of the world, you'll understand. A hungry man can't be choosy but I couldn't stomach sharing that revolting woman's bed. So after a couple of days, I walked out on her and took her loose money and jewels as a parting present. I hid from the police for weeks on end and then managed to bribe a *passeur* who smuggled me across the frontier into Belgium."

That kind of story would be more credible to the Gestapo than any tale of honest endeavor. All agents from that time onward who were sent on secret missions had their "story within a story" carefully prepared before they left. There is little doubt that many lives were saved as a result.

Of all the men and women agents who underwent my examination before going on active service only one sailed through with nonchalant ease and without making the slightest mistake. He was the perfect secret agent and although he entered Occupied Belgium on many special missions he never once fell foul of the Gestapo. In fact he did not even come under suspicion.

When I was told that a Monsieur Jean Dufour was coming to see me I expected the usual intelligent, healthy-looking young man. But when the door opened, my eyes

103

goggled and my lower jaw dropped in surprise. An officer walked in, accompanied by what I can only call the travesty of a human being. This object looked like a typical village idiot. Not only was he deformed but his cheeks and lower jaw were three times the usual size. His pale blue eyes were vacant, without the slightest glimmer of sense. His lips were slack and wet and saliva dribbled from one corner of his mouth. He leered at me, grimaced foolishly and then broke into a high-pitched giggle.

"What the hell is this?" I demanded. "Are you trying to pull my leg?"

The officer smiled. "May I introduce Monsieur Jean Dufour," he said. "If he passes your tests he will become a carrier carrying money to our agents in France and Belgium."

"He doesn't need Counter-Intelligence tests by the look of him," I remarked. "A psychiatrist would be more in his line. Still, I'm at your service, so here goes."

I turned to the pitiable moron who giggled again, then put out a stubby, dirty finger and gently touched the inkwell on my desk as though it were something beautiful and strange. Then he looked up—and winked at me. For a moment shrewd intelligence flashed across his vacant features, and then disappeared.

"How old are you, Dufour?" I asked abruptly in Flemish.

"How old am I?" he giggled. He patted me on the shoulder. "How old am I, old man? How should I know?" He threw his head back and roared with laughter.

I pressed him with further questions. Where was he

104

born? How would he know? Where had he lived? "Me, old man? I don't live anywhere." The same slobbering laugh.

I glared at him. "Come on, you aren't fooling me. You must live somewhere," I snapped.

But he was not impressed. Giggling, he spluttered, "I live on *les grandes routes*—the main roads—of Belgium. In the fields and the woods—the haystacks."

"What does your father do for a living?"

He scratched his matted hair and laughed even louder. A spray of saliva wet both my desk and myself. "That's a good one, old man. My father—he is crazy, a loony—"

If this maniac accused his father of being mad, then indeed the latter must be a sad case. "Why?" I persisted.

"Why? Because the old fool works!"

"And you don't believe in working?"

He thumped his misshapen chest in self-approval. "Me work? Why should I? I sleep, mostly in the fields. I dine better than a duke. Where there's a farm there are cows and when the farmer's not looking, there's free milk. Hens are friendly and you give one a little squeeze round the neck. Put it in the pot and there's your supper." He patted his stomach in memory of alfresco free meals in the past.

There was something infectious about his simple gaiety. I found myself smiling as I asked him whether he had ever attended school. No, he had never been to school but, he added grandly, he could write his name.

"Let me see you do it!"

He took up my pen as though it might bite him and

105

rolled back his ragged cuffs. Drawing back his arm like a violinist about to attack the Beethoven concerto, he leaned over the paper, head cocked on one side and tongue protruding. With a fine flourish he scratched a wobbly "X" on the paper. "There," he said in triumph, "Jean Dufour at your service."

For over an hour I kept at him but had to admit myself beaten in the end. Not three words of useful information did I achieve.

"Take him away," I said to his sponsor. "Send him to Belgium whenever you like. The Gestapo will never break him. Before they've finished he'll be breaking them. After the Belgian police have arrested him for the umpteenth time and then let him go, every policeman will turn and run like mad when they see him approaching. He'll be the curse of the whole police department. He's a genius!"

The intelligence officer grinned. "He'll be on his way pretty soon. He's a big enough headache to the London police already. He's supposed to be billeted in a very nice flat in the Edgware Road but it doesn't suit him. Every night he's off to Hyde Park to sleep out on the grass."

They left my office and Dufour grinned an impudent farewell. That was the last I saw of him in the misshapen flesh but I followed his subsequent career with great interest. The first time he was dropped into Belgium by parachute he carried four hundred pounds in money for one of our agents in Brussels. Not forty-eight hours later the message arrived. "Mission accomplished." Again and again he was dropped, he completed his task, was brought out and

106

made ready for yet another mission. Never once did he fail to keep a rendezvous at the appointed hour, however close the police or the Gestapo might be. In all he must have carried thousands of pounds to various agents in Belgium yet there was never a penny missing.

This illiterate, apparently witless petty poacher-*cum*-vagabond was the supreme secret agent. He succeeded time and again where men of superior intelligence and physique would sooner or later have failed. This tattered scarecrow of a man was an invaluable asset to the British Secret Service.

I should like to meet him again. He would get the best chicken dinner in London—and the chicken would have been paid for, not poached!

107

CHAPTER VII

Patience Is a Virtue

1

WHATEVER their faults, the Germans must be given credit for thoroughness and organizing ability. During the first hectic months after the Fall of France and the occupation of the Low Countries, many thousands of refugees managed to escape to England in the confusion of the times. Some arrived by boat, setting out by night for the dash to safety from a quiet creek which might be anywhere along that indented line of seacoast from Norway to Brittany. Others traveled by land southward until they reached the Pyrenees, and then climbed the frontier into Spain whence, if they could avoid Franco's policemen, they would eventually reach Portugal and await passage from Lisbon. Gradually, as the Gestapo and the German Security Police sealed off the coast line and military patrols were established along the hundreds of miles of shores, escaping refugees became fewer in number. It needed not only courage but seamanship of a high order and a large slice of luck to risk the crossing in an open boat. Aerial reconnaissance over the Channel might easily spot a boatload of refugees and a machine-gun burst from a Luftwaffe aircraft swooping low would soon put an end to the refugees'

108

chances. There were also high-powered launches carrying out coastal patrols that could not easily be evaded by rowing boats and small sailing ships. Capture might mean summary death by drowning or death by execution afterward or at the best a long spell of imprisonment in a concentration camp. Thus, during 1941 and 1942, the numbers of refugees reaching England declined to a small stream from the floods that had arrived in the first six months after Dunkirk.

But the Germans realized before long that by effectively shutting off the inhabitants of Occupied Europe from escape to England they were equally shutting themselves off from information. The man who locks himself in a room may keep concealed from the outside world but equally well the outside world is concealed from him. The Germans desperately needed information about England, its rate of recovery from the hard blows of Dunkirk and the air raids, its troop dispositions and build-up, its plans for a possible return to the Continent. Aerial reconnaissance and photography was one means of securing part of this information but it was not wholly accurate and always required confirmation from the ground.

The Germans soon hit on the solution to the problem. Whenever they had wind of an attempted escape to England they would not necessarily arrest the conspirators. It might pay them to let the attempt go forward *after* they had managed to slip a spy into the party of refugees. One spy in a bunch of genuine escapers—or "escapees" as they were called in the brutal and ungrammatical jargon that disfigured wartime England's communiqués and official pronouncements—would be less conspicuous than if he arrived on his own. The main fact that his companions were demonstrably genuine and did not suspect his credentials, since he too would have apparently played his part in organizing the escape and confronting the dangers that faced them all, made it more likely that his testimony would be corroborated by the other witnesses to his escape.

This solution of the problem had one other virtue from the German point of view. An agent who entered England via Lisbon might arrive many months after he had first set out. Knowing the ropes, it would not take him long to reach Lisbon but once there he would have to join the queue of refugees of all nationalities waiting for visas and then for passages in ships that could only carry a small percentage of the swarms who eagerly awaited their departure. Such a spy would not risk drawing attention on himself by "jumping the queue" or using influence to advance his sailing date. All he could do was take his turn and wait patiently so that when he did eventually reach England and if he managed to elude the Counter-Intelligence interrogation his orders might well be completely out of date. The situation he had come to report on might have changed entirely and, unless he could obtain fresh instructions which was not an easy task at the best of times, he was risking his neck to no purpose.

On the other hand crossing the Channel by boat would take only a few days at the most so that the German agent who managed to slip through the Counter-Intelligence net

110

would be on the job without delay. From the German angle it was a good plan and if it meant losing agents at an accelerated rate, although this was not a foregone conclusion, they realized that no one can fight a war without suffering casualties.

The British were not slow to realize that the most up-to-date information came from refugees escaping by boat. The preliminary interrogations of such escapees were conducted by Royal Air Force intelligence officers. Any news of operational value was flashed to Bomber and Fighter Command and could be acted on at once. There might be information as recent as yesterday on troop concentrations or secret factories making special war equipment or even of a military conference at some hide-out where senior officers would be present. It was obviously essential for such items to reach the R.A.F. "briefing rooms" without any delay.

These R.A.F. intelligence officers were usually first class at the job but one must remember that their job did not include spy-catching. They were out to obtain information of aerial importance and they naturally left the security side to Counter-Intelligence, who would in any case have to "vet" all the escapees after they had passed through the hands of the R.A.F.

One morning in the early spring of 1942 the telephone rang in my office at the Royal Victoria Patriotic School. At the other end was an R.A.F. intelligence officer, an old acquaintance of mine, but on this occasion he was far from cheerful. He told me that he had just finished interrogating

111

three Dutchmen who had arrived in a small boat off the southeast coast. At any rate, two of them had been interrogated but the third appeared to be a lunatic—or at least so hysterical with joy at escaping to safety that no sense could be got out of him. One moment he would weep tears of relief and the next he would shout and scream and sing wild songs of praise to his Heavenly Maker. Apart from the fact that he was Dutch and his name appeared to be Dronkers, the intelligence officer could get no sense from him. Would I like to carry on from there?

I would. A few hours later Mynheer Dronkers was brought into my room. He was tall and very thin, with the skin stretched so tight over his cheekbones that they seemed about to burst through. He had white hair and dark intelligent eyes. Normally he would be a soberly dressed and dignified petty official, a little self-important perhaps but full of solid worth and honesty. But the R.A.F. officer had not exaggerated. Dronkers was indeed beside himself. He burst into my room like a whirling dervish, waving his arms and skipping to and fro, shrieking in his cracked voice an old Dutch patriotic song. He embraced me fervently and shook my hands until my arms ached. And when he was not singing he was babbling a paean of praise to the Deity who had watched over him so well.

I managed to quiet him down a little but as soon as I congratulated him on his escape he was off again. It was nerve-racking to see an elderly, dignified man so completely out of control and, realizing that one must be severe with cases of hysteria, I spoke to him sharply. "Now look

112

here, you're glad to be safe and we're glad for your sake. But this demonstration is becoming childish. And worse than childish, it's selfish. You owe it to your less fortunate countrymen who have not yet escaped from German clutches to calm down and tell me exactly how you planned this escape from Holland. You may well have hit on some method which could be used again to save many more Dutchmen who want to escape. So get a grip on your feelings and calm down. Do you hear?"

He nodded. Gradually he managed to restrain his emotion and then sat down limply in a chair on the other side of my desk. With that strange and sudden reverse that often occurs in cases of extreme shock, he became almost apathetic as he told me the story of his escape.

He had been married for over twenty-five years, he said. There were no children. He and his wife lived in a tiny flat in The Hague. He was a postal clerk and naturally the salary for such a humble position was a meager one. They had always had a struggle to make both ends meet by pinching and scraping and doing without the luxuries of life. After the German occupation in 1940 their circumstances went from bad to worse. Prices went up and up and all the staple items of food and clothing became almost impossible to get. Life which had always been a drudgery now became a nightmare and his wife was wasting away before his eyes. In despair and for his wife's sake—and he blushed in admitting it—he went into the black market. It was illegal but he had no option. Straightaway he found himself prospering. Money was to be had for the asking

113

and from the depths of poverty he began to emerge into prosperity.

It was too easy and, being a cautious man, he realized that this sudden wealth could hardly go on forever. In the back of his mind he knew that one day trouble would catch up with him but as the weeks went by and the money rolled in he thrust the warning thoughts away from him. Then out of the blue disaster threatened. One evening last January a friend called to tip him off that the Gestapo were after him. They were making big efforts to round up black market operators in Holland and so put an end to this illegal trading which was endangering their regime. Dronkers had either been found out or betrayed but, whatever the cause, the Gestapo were on his trail.

The penalty for being a black marketeer caught by the Gestapo was death. He and his wife both knew that. The friend who had come to warn him said that there was only one way out. If he stayed in Holland the Gestapo were bound to catch up with him, probably sooner than later. He must escape to England. After some discussion his wife agreed that he must go. There was little chance that the Gestapo would harm her in his absence, since his black market activities had luckily been carried out away from their home and at that time the Germans were behaving in Holland with a certain "correctness." They would hardly make a hostage out of the innocent wife.

This invaluable friend suggested that Dronkers should make his way to a well-known café in Rotterdam, the Café

114

Atlanta, where he would probably find someone to help him on his journey.

At this point in the story I nodded. I remembered the Café Atlanta myself.

Dronkers went on with his account and although he told it in a rambling and sometimes incoherent way it emerged as a fairly straightforward story. He went to Rotterdam next day and called at the café. Luck was with him. He fell into casual conversation with a man called "Hans" and after a while blurted out the confidential facts that the Gestapo were after him. He had come to Rotterdam in the desperate hope that he could find a boat to take him to England.

Hans, smiling broadly, told him that he could not have met a better person to help him. He, Hans, was employed by a Rotterdam businessman who was in charge of the distribution of petrol to ships in the harbor. The businessman owned a seaworthy boat of which Hans was the skipper. Seeing that Dronkers was in a mess and to outwit the stinking Gestapo, Hans was prepared to sell him the boat. Like good Dutch businessmen they haggled for a while over the price and finally agreed on the sum of forty pounds. It was the most that Dronkers could afford.

They evolved a simple plan. Hans would stock the boat with sufficient petrol for the trip to England. No trouble here because through his job he could always get hold of petrol without arousing anyone's suspicions. Dronkers would be smuggled on board and hidden away in the cabin. Then Hans would take the boat through the locks and past

115

the German sentries who all knew him well and were used to seeing him come and go. Besides, he held a special pass authorizing him to make such trips. Once the boat was out of sight of the harbor, Hans could be put ashore further down the coast and from then on it was up to Dronkers to navigate himself to England. If he kept a westward course he was bound to hit it.

"That was the plan," said Dronkers, "and, praise God, it worked. But not before various things happened which nearly scared me out of my wits. I had a young friend who was desperately anxious to get to England and finally agreed to take him along. And then he had a friend who was equally keen to go. I didn't like the idea of having a third person on that small boat but in the end I gave in.

"There we were, the three of us, crouched in that tiny cabin which smelled dreadfully. It seemed a lifetime before we cast off and then an age as we crept through the locks. We hardly dared breathe when we heard Hans at the helm laughing and joking with the German sentries. And then the engine went louder and we could feel the boat gathering speed and rocking a bit. We were in the open sea.

"When the boat was nearing the Hook, Hans ran it ashore. I paid him the forty pounds we had agreed on and I thanked him from the bottom of my heart. After all, I owe him my life. Forty pounds was not much to pay for that."

I nodded and lit another cigarette.

Dronkers choked down his emotion. His eyes were full

116

of tears. "There's not much more to tell you, sir," he went on. "Mind you, it was not all plain sailing from then on. I was not much of a hand at navigating nor were the others. The first thing we did was to run onto a sandbank. It took us hours to get afloat again and all the time that terrible searchlight kept traveling backward and forward"—he waved his hands from side to side—"across the sandbank where we were stuck. It was a miracle we weren't spotted. . . ."

He breathed a deep and very audible sigh. Then he sprang up and, with a renewed attack of his wild joy, jigged his feet and tossed his hands in the air, shouting, "But thank God it's all over now! Here I am, safe and sound in England! My troubles are over!"

I crushed out my cigarette in an ash tray. "Dronkers," I said, "I have the suspicion that your real troubles are just beginning."

2

There was silence for a long moment. He sat down and stared at me. I stared back.

"Excuse me, sir," he said, "but I must have misheard you."

"No, Dronkers," I went on. "I spoke clearly enough. In my view your troubles are by no means over. You have just told me a most interesting story. It reminded me of the writings of that famous American writer, Edgar Allan Poe. But, if you remember, he called his stories *Tales of Mystery and Imagination*. That's where the similarity comes in.

117

Your story was certainly mysterious and, I gather, straight from your imagination. In simple words—I suspect you made it all up. Now, how about telling me the truth instead?"

He stared at me again. His tongue darted across his dry lips. And then his blank astonishment gave way to anger.

"I beg your pardon, sir. Are you accusing me of lying? It's a monstrous charge. I find myself gravely insulted!"

I leaned forward. "Tell me, Dronkers, why should your friend Hans want to commit suicide?"

He blinked. "Suicide? What do you mean?"

"That Rotterdam businessman—the one who owned the boat. He must have missed it by now, don't you think? The German sentries could tell him that Hans had taken it out of the harbor but now Hans has come back but the boat has disappeared. It seems odd, doesn't it? The businessman won't like to lose this good boat in wartime when boats are hard to replace. He'll probably put the Gestapo onto Hans—and what story can Hans tell which will satisfy them? The Gestapo can be pretty tough when they like."

Dronkers stared at me again.

I went on. "Did it never occur to you—or to Hans himself—that he was virtually committing suicide—and all for the miserable sum of forty pounds?"

Dronkers shook his head. There were tears in his eyes. "Good God," he muttered, "we hadn't thought of that."

"Further," I said, "a man who goes to Rotterdam to find a boat that will take him secretly to England would never visit the only smart luxury café that wasn't flattened by the

118

bombing. Now why did you do that? You we
and only place in Rotterdam where you would
not to meet any sailors. Why didn't you go to a
side pub where there'd always be plenty of sailors?

Dronkers assumed an air of much resignation. "W
you believe me or not, sir, I have told you the truth."

"Have you? Truth may often be strange but this pas
the bounds of belief. How do you explain that in this posh
crowded café you should bump into the one man—probably in all Holland—who could help you? And weren't you
taking an awful risk in blurting out your story to a complete stranger? He might easily have been a Gestapo agent,
mightn't he? And, above all, how could a smart fellow like
Hans risk certain imprisonment, torture and death for a
miserable forty pounds? Give me a satisfactory answer to
all those questions and perhaps I'll believe you."

Dronkers sighed. "I can only repeat that I have told you
the truth, sir."

I shook my head. "Dronkers, I know exactly what you
are. A liar. I even know who has sent you on this errand.
Herr Strauch of the German Secret Service, wasn't it? I'll
give you exactly twenty-four hours to think things over.
Tomorrow at this time you will come and see me again—
and perhaps you'll tell me the truth then."

"I have already told you the truth, sir."

As I rang for the guards to come and escort him away,
I looked at him with renewed respect. He was going to be
tougher to break than I had at first suspected. He was so
convinced of his rectitude that for a moment I wondered

119

whether his story might not just be true. But I quickly dismissed the thought. He was a spy and I was going to make him confess it.

Just before he left the room he fired a parting shot. He would write to the highest authorities and let them know that they were harboring a Himmler. (He did indeed write those letters, one to Queen Wilhelmina, one to the King of England and one to Mr. Winston Churchill, but they were never delivered to the august addressees.)

As the door closed behind him I sat back and lit a cigarette. I ran over the outlines of his story in my mind. More than ever, I was certain that he had told a tissue of lies and that he was a spy. I resolved to make him admit it but I did not then realize that the task would take thirteen days and nights of unremitting labor.

3

I have already stressed the importance of searching the belongings of all refugees. Timmermans, for example, would never have been apprehended if he had not carried those three damning pieces of evidence in his wallet. It has been my experience that every spy carries something incriminating either on his person or in his luggage. It may be insignificant or some object that would only be noted by the trained searcher but it is always there for the finding. A spy has two jobs to perform. He has first of all to find the information he is looking for and then he has to pass it on to the quarter where it will be best used or acted upon. To achieve this twofold task he usually requires an *aide-*

mémoire consisting either of notes on the information required or perhaps the foreign address to which he must send that information and often notes on both points. He may also carry the means, such as a microcamera, for passing the information in a secret manner.

If a spy possesses sufficient resolution and strength of character and if he has been properly trained, no amount of interrogation by itself will make him confess. Only physical torture would achieve that end and, as I have already explained, British Counter-Intelligence draws the line well short of torture.

So I fell into a certain routine with Mynheer Dronkers. Every day I made him repeat his story over and over again. Every day I pointed out the same huge improbabilities and asked him the same point-blank questions. And every day like clockwork I got the same unvarying answer, "I have told you the truth, sir."

I was too busy during the daytime with other cases apart from his to spend time on searching his belongings. So each night I took a neat parcel of them back to my Chelsea flat and after dinner, while often the air-raid sirens howled and sometimes bombs came crashing down in the neighborhood, I worked at the contents of the parcel until the small hours of the morning. On a bare table under a powerful electric light I placed his ordinary belongings and then concentrated on each in turn.

First the silver watch and chain. I examined each link of the chain under a microscope. There was no incriminating sign on any one. I took the watch to pieces, scruti-

121

nized the inside and outside of the case, examined the gears for telltale scratches, removed the mainspring, held the microscope over each jewel. I found nothing.

Next came a pocketknife. I peered for a long time at the blade and the bone handle, covering each millimeter systematically. Then I stripped the bone from the handle and punched out each of the retaining screws. Again I found nothing.

The next item was a packet of cheap Dutch cigarettes, "North State." I stripped each one, tested the flimsy paper for writing in invisible ink, then sifted the harsh tobacco. I tested the crumpled paper packet inside and out. I could find nothing. Yawning, I rubbed my smarting eyes and decided to call off the search in favor of a few hours' sleep for what remained of the night.

Next day after another fruitless interrogation of the sullen, resentful Dronkers, I decided to try another expedient. The two men who had escaped with him, though an oddly assorted pair, had both been found genuine. One had been a postal clerk in The Hague and thus a colleague of Dronkers. He was a thin, fragile little fellow with a persistent sniffle, a case of chronic catarrh and possibly tuberculosis as well. But a bright spirit burned inside his meager frame and he wanted desperately to volunteer for the Free Dutch Army. The other was a half-caste Malayan Dutch and although he was prone to exaggerations which sometimes strayed across the boundaries of truth, we had finally found him harmless enough.

I sent for this latter talkative man and when he and

122

Dronkers were assembled in my office, I made some excuse for leaving them. I hurried to the commandant's room across the corridor and listened to their conversation which was picked up by the microphone hidden in the plain white shade of the electric light. Dronkers answered the other man's voluble questions and statements with monosyllables or grunts. Nothing in what either of them said or left unsaid was in any way incriminating. After listening for nearly ten minutes I realized that nothing would be gained from this method and so returned to my room. Dismissing the half-caste, I carried on interrogating Dronkers but again to no effect. To any statement or question I might put to him he transposed that monotonous sentence, "I have told you the truth, sir."

And so the days and the nights passed with no results gained either by questioning Dronkers by day nor by examining his belongings by night. I had now got on to the newspapers and maps he had brought and I spent hours at my fireside poring over every square inch of paper, patiently and scrupulously testing both sides under the microscope and with special chemicals. There were times as I lit yet another cigarette and sipped yet another cup of coffee when I wondered whether I was wasting all these hours to no purpose. Could it be that my overzealousness had led me astray and, if Dronkers were innocent, I was searching in a haystack for a needle that did not exist? Had I, who had always warned my junior colleagues against forming impressions and allowing their intuitions to carry them away, been guilty of such an error myself?

123

The next morning I confronted Dronkers again. I accused him of being a spy and a traitor to his country. And his only reply was the same sentence which rang in my ears every time I saw or thought of him.

"I have told you the truth, sir." He said it in a tired, resigned way, almost as though he were as tired of me as I indeed was of him. Perhaps he was.

"Now, look here, Dronkers, you have stuck to your guns very well. I congratulate you on your tenacity. But you don't really think that all this stubbornness is going to get you anywhere, do you? Don't you realize that you will never get out of here alive? You are a spy and I know you are a spy. I can keep on asking you questions longer than you can keep on giving me the same answer. Sooner or later, you will have to give in. Why do you prolong your own agony? Why don't you admit the truth that you are a spy and put an end to all this questioning?"

There was a moment of complete silence inside the room, marred only by the sound of footsteps in the corridor outside and by the distant humming of traffic passing through Clapham. Dronkers stood up slowly and stared at me. He raised one hand, the index finger pointing to the ceiling. In spite of my outward control I could feel my muscles turning with excitement. Was this the long-awaited breaking point?

"Sir," said Dronkers impressively, "in the name of the God I worship and in the name of my dead father whom I loved and who is assuredly in Heaven, I swear to you

124

solemnly that I am faithful to my country and to the House of Orange. I am not a spy."

My muscles relaxed and I leaned back in my chair. I said—I could say—nothing.

Suddenly Dronkers sat down and burst into tears. For over a quarter of an hour his shoulders twitched and fresh sobs broke out. I sat there looking at him as he slowly regained his composure.

"All the same, Dronkers, you are a spy and I am determined to prove it."

4

On the twelfth evening I had come to the last of Dronkers' possessions. It was a bulky copy of Kramer's Dutch-English dictionary. The covers and flyleaves were stained by the salt water of the sea. Somewhere within those seven hundred pages lurked the clue to the Dronkers case—or else I had wasted nearly a fortnight of concentrated work on attempting to pin guilt onto an innocent man. There lay the dictionary on my table. Nearby was a large ash tray piled already to overflowing with the innumerable cigarette ends I had crushed into it. Outside the night was hideous with the sounds of a severe air raid, the repeated sharp barking of antiaircraft guns and the shriek and thud of falling bombs.

Lighting up another cigarette and sipping from a cup of bitter black coffee, I examined the outside of the covers, peeling off the binding and even cutting it down the spine of the book. I found no evidence. There was only one thing

125

left to do. Every word on every line of a closely-printed dictionary, seven hundred pages in length, had to be scrutinized under the microscope.

I began this wearing task and the hours went by as I turned page after page. The all clear went. Switching off the light I closed my aching eyes and went over to pull the heavy black-out curtain. The sky was red with the light of burning fires and also with the approaching dawn. An air-raid warden, helmet in hand, went stumbling past with fatigue written on every line of his body. His face was black with the grime of fires and debris. I sipped a glass of iced water, then returned to the dictionary.

Page followed page and I had found nothing. I was now more than halfway through the book and as I turned each page and focused the microscope on its successor I knew that another chance of proving Dronkers' guilt had been eliminated.

And then, as I scrutinized page 432, I sat back and gasped with relief. There was the clue—a tiny pinprick under a capital letter "F." At last I knew the method by which Dronkers had worked and I was certain that there would be other fatal pinpricks under other letters in the remaining pages of the dictionary. There were. I jotted them down in pencil as they occurred. Fortunately they were in their proper sequence or else I should have had two tricky anagrams to solve. At last all the pinpricks were noted on a piece of scribbling paper. They formed two names and addresses to which Dronkers was to have sent whatever information he managed to secure. The first was

126

in Stockholm; it read: Froeken Annette Yschale, Grev-magnigatan, 13-V. The other was in Lisbon and read: Fernando Laurero, Rua Souza Martin.

Relieved that the work of thirteen days had culminated successfully and yet perhaps a little disappointed because the attainment of a goal that has been striven for desperately is often something of an anticlimax, I snatched a few hours' sleep. On my return to the Royal Victoria Patriotic School, I sent for Dronkers. When he entered the room I noticed for the first time how old he seemed and how bent. He slumped down in the wicker chair on the other side of my desk and watched me apathetically. He was obviously as bored as I was with our daily meetings but, unlike me, he did not realize that this was to be the last of them.

I took from a pocket the piece of paper on which were written the names and addresses of Dronkers' two foreign "contacts." I unfolded it and smoothed out the creases before placing it on the table.

"Dronkers," I said, "for the hundredth time, do you admit that you are a spy?"

The response came automatically, as though I had pressed the right button. "I have told you the truth, sir."

I turned the damning piece of paper upside down so that he could read its contents. In the still room my voice sank to a whisper. "Dronkers, you were born a Dutchman but you will be hanged as a traitor. Read those two lines. Now will you confess to being a spy?"

It was the end. Dronkers realized that the game was up. His stubborn resistance crumbled. He broke down and

127

confessed everything. Yes, he was a spy. He had indeed been sent by Herr Strauch, that pillar of the German Secret Service who frequented the Café Atlanta in Rotterdam. "Hans" had of course been in league with the Germans. The other passengers were entirely innocent and had only been brought along to give semblance to Dronkers' story.

Soon a stenographer was taking down Dronkers' rambling statement which needed only a few questions and prompting to reveal all the sordid details. In a matter of minutes the confession was typed out and he had signed it. The case was complete. Professionally I had no further interest in him but from a personal point of view I wanted to find the mainspring that had driven this petty official, the epitome of the rather smug bourgeois, to treachery.

"Tell me, Dronkers, what made you do it? What made you, an honest man, stoop to this unspeakable crime against your country?"

He sat there, utterly abject, with all resistance gone. Slowly and stumblingly he told me the story and something like pity stirred in me as I listened. This man, grown gray and worn before his time with pinching and scraping, who had never known the finer things of life, had one aim which was completely unselfish and even noble. It was his utter devotion to his wife. He had indeed meddled with black market activities but not with any success as he had previously claimed. He had been eventually faced with downright poverty and starvation which he could have endured for himself but could not bear to see his wife suffering. So he had volunteered to spy for the Germans as a last resort.

128

They had promised to pay his wife the meager sum equivalent to £15 per month for three months and, on his return, a job for himself worth £200 a year—if he returned. And he would have to make his own way back without any assistance from them. It was a good bargain—from the German point of view.

And here he was, only a fortnight after he had left Holland on his desperate errand. As he told me haltingly that he had risked everything for his wife's sake, I believed him, for the first time in thirteen days.

5

He appeared before Mr. Justice Wrottesley in the Central Criminal Court on the thirteenth, sixteenth and seventeenth of November, 1942. He was condemned to death.

On the fourteenth of December he appealed against the sentence. The appeal was heard before the Lord Chief Justice and was ultimately rejected.

On New Year's Eve, 1942, he was hanged in Wandsworth Prison.

CHAPTER VIII

Never Say Die

1

AFTER the Normandy landing I was ordered to go to the Continent with a staff of six security officers as head of the Netherlands Counter-Intelligence Mission, attached to Supreme Headquarters Allied Expeditionary Forces. In that capacity I was given the task, jointly with British Security, of "cleaning up" and then maintaining the security of the lines of communication behind the advancing Allied Armies which by then had broken out of the Normandy bridgehead and were rolling across France and Belgium into Holland.

It was not an easy job for a man on the eve of his fifty-fifth birthday. Living under field service conditions with irregular meals, journeys by car along bumpy, shell-pocked roads, snatching a few hours' sleep without the luxury of undressing was in itself quite arduous. I do not want the reader to accuse me of false heroics or self-pity, because my lot was as nothing compared with that of the front-line troops whose privations and danger were ten times as great. But I was no longer a young man and although I could keep going I had lost that priceless advantage of youth—the elasticity of body and spirit which enables an exhausted

130

man to regain his normal strength after only a few hours of rest.

There were also enough jobs to do which would have filled the twenty-four hours of the day twice over and still have left a surplus. In every town that was liberated there were accusations and counteraccusations that this or that petty official was a collaborator. Everyone who had an old score to pay off would come forward with the most realistic charges of helping the enemy directed against some political or business opponent. All these charges had to be investigated, questions had to be asked, interrogations and cross-examinations undertaken. Sooner or later the truth, or an approximation to the truth, would be reached but it all took precious time, and meanwhile the unheard cases were piling up. The Germans, true to form and tenacious to the last, left saboteurs and spies behind their retreating forces, with orders to blow up this bridge or that arsenal or merely to report back the progress and order of battle of the advancing Allies. Such men and women had to be rounded up and rendered harmless. Over and above my normal duties, I had the added excitement and strain of being on the fringe of a case which turned out to be the biggest I was ever to handle and which I propose to discuss in detail in a later chapter.

Then, to add to my troubles, my hand-picked staff of six security officers began to emulate the "ten little Indian boys." The American forces, who were in desperate need of additional trained men on the security side, borrowed two of them and when I bade them "Au revoir" it should have

131

been "Good-by." I never saw either of them again during the rest of the war. Then I was ordered to "lend" two more to the British Armies and this was another case of "hail and farewell." Finally the Canadian Army secured my two survivors and although I tried time and again to put pressure on the higher authorities to effect their return I was unsuccessful. So, single-handed, I was forced to undertake the work for which seven of us had previously been woefully inadequate. Looking back, I realize that if I had been able to plan my staff on the lavish lines engaged by the bigger Headquarters I could have found sufficient employment for at least one hundred officers and men. Yet for several weeks, without proper transport or the seniority and authority which would have smoothed my path, I had to scour the hundreds of miles behind the broad front of the armies which by then were advancing swiftly into Holland.

By the time that S.H.A.E.F. had been set up in Brussels and I had reached Eindhoven in southern Holland, I felt myself to be on the verge of a nervous breakdown. I had lost nearly two stone in weight—and I am not normally a man who carries much spare flesh. I was in the grip of a ceaseless headache by day, accentuated by raging insomnia by night. My appetite was gone as though it had never existed. Neuritis made it an agony for me to stay in one position for any length of time and yet I was too mentally and physically tired to want to move about. I felt that I was at the end of my tether and in a short while nature confirmed my suspicions. On December 22, 1944, I collapsed.

A friend rushed me to Security Headquarters at Brussels and from there I was sent to a Military Hospital for examination. The specialist, a major, gave me the most thorough and grueling examination I have ever undergone. It lasted for an hour and a half, during which time he asked me all the details of my family medical history, questions on my way of life, my antecedents and details of many other subjects which to my lay mind did not seem particularly relevant. He probed and tapped and prodded me all over, examining my heart, lungs, stomach, back, indeed it seemed every organ I possessed. As a specialist in other kinds of examinations I metaphorically took off my hat to this doctor for his thoroughness.

As I was dressing again afterward, he scribbled out his diagnosis on a piece of paper, signed it and sealed it in an envelope which he handed to me. He said in an offhand way that I ought to report back to England without delay and, when I arrived, I was to hand the letter to my own doctor.

I had interrogated too many people to be put off by his apparently casual air. Besides, as most of us know, when one's own state of health is the topic of the moment, one becomes hypersensitive to nuances of speech and manner.

"I am not a child, Doctor," I said. "Into the bargain I hope that whatever else I may be, I am not a coward. Tell me straight what is the matter with me."

133

He hummed and hawed and muttered something about professional etiquette.

"Etiquette be damned," I said. "I am bound to find out when I reach London, aren't I? Well then, tell me what's wrong now."

He shrugged his shoulders. "All right. In my opinion you are suffering from an advanced case of cancer in the abdomen with secondaries in both lungs. I didn't want to tell you but you asked for it."

At the word "cancer" my heart seemed to stop beating. There was something so final about that word.

"Is it—too late for an operation?" I asked.

He looked me straight in the face and then nodded. "I'm afraid so," he said.

"How long do you give me then?"

"It's hard to tell. With some people it takes a good time, with others not."

"How about me?"

"Well, if you press me, I should say—two months, perhaps three. But it's impossible to say exactly." He broke off and gave me a wry smile which was all sympathy. "I'm sorry, old chap, it's damned hard to break the news when it's this way. But you did insist on my telling you the truth. Good-by—and good luck."

He shook my hand and somehow I managed to walk outside into the fresh air. Suddenly I realized the keenness of perception that comes to a condemned man. The very air had a nip and a tingle that I had forgotten. As I stood there, drawing deep breaths into those lungs that were already, it seemed, disintegrating under the deadly, burrowing disease, the sharp outlines of the houses, the rumble of military lorries, the colored scarves and shawls of the Belgian women passing by took on a strange clarity. In two days' time it would be Christmas Eve. And then I realized. It would be the last Christmas I should see on this earth. Every beat of my pulse was like a drumbeat marching me down that road and I was very near the end of it.

For hours I wandered through the cold streets of Brussels in a daze. It seemed like a nightmare from which I would presently wake up, safe and sound, but the sharp corners of the envelope which held my "death sentence" reminded me of reality every time my fingers strayed to my pocket. Somehow I reached Headquarters and put in an application for an air passage back to London. I wanted to leave at once, like an animal that makes for its own burrow at the end, but as it was so near Christmas all homebound planes were booked up. The earliest day I could leave was the twenty-seventh of December. I shrugged my shoulders cynically when I got over the initial disappointment. Let the dying make way for the living at this time of celebration. What did a day here or a day there matter to a man who could not fly away from his fate?

I returned to the mess to which I was attached. Being posted back to the United Kingdom at such short notice needed explaining, at least to the few good friends I had. Bad news travels fast and soon every officer in the mess was aware of my reason for leaving them in a few days' time. The embarrassed sympathy, so inarticulate and touch-

135

ing, of those decent Englishmen is difficult to describe. All I can say is that this was certainly the worst Christmas I have ever spent and it was effectively spoiled for the majority of my companions. I was indeed "the death's head at the feast."

On December 27 I flew back to London. My first move was to arrange an appointment with my own doctor. I presented him with the specialist's diagnosis and he then examined me. After a while he asked, "I suppose your Army specialist gave you an X-ray before he reached his conclusion?"

"No," I said.

"What? He didn't X-ray you? How on earth could he reach a definite conclusion on a grave matter without giving you a barium meal and then an X-ray? Frankly, Pinto, from this preliminary examination I can find no trace of your having cancer but of course I must stress the fact that it's impossible to be dogmatic without more detailed tests, including X-rays. At least, to a mere harassed civilian medico it's impossible. Apparently the Army takes a different view." He grinned.

Somewhere within me a flicker of hope was beginning to melt the icy numbness that had possessed me. "What happens now?" I asked.

"I'll arrange for you to be given a detailed examination by a Harley Street specialist," he said. "The sooner the better. Could you be available tomorrow, for instance?"

I nodded. I could hardly trust myself to speak.

And so it was arranged. On the following day I visited

136

the Harley Street specialist and after I had managed to swallow the nauseating barium meal, I was X-rayed in the greatest detail. Two days later, I was summoned to see my own doctor again. Sick with waiting and still wondering what the final answer would be, I walked into his consulting room. I began to realize how the condemned man feels on the morning of his execution when he knows that a last-minute reprieve has been urgently sought.

My doctor greeted me heartily. He was rubbing his hands with glee. "Well, Pinto," he said, "I'm the bearer of good tidings. No doctor likes to disagree publicly with his learned colleague but I must tell you that your Army specialist has come a cropper this time. There's not a trace of cancer in that system of yours. Certainly you're suffering from complete exhaustion and nervous debility. Any fool can see that. But there's nothing organically the matter with you. A couple of months' complete rest will see you one hundred per cent fit again and hopping about like a sparrow. Well, say something. Anyone would think you wanted to die."

I could say nothing. In that moment I knew the sensation of being reprieved on the eve of one's execution.

2

For the next three months I enjoyed a complete rest. Once the Ardennes offensive, that last despairing effort at attack by the Germans, was checked, then broken, it seemed inevitable that the war in Europe was grinding to a halt. I realized that there would be plenty of jobs awaiting

137

my return but for a short while I shrugged off thoughts of the future. I was content to relax and let the days drift by, knowing that this was the first period of inactivity, mental and physical, that had come my way for nearly five and a half years.

Meanwhile I gathered that the news of the impending death of Lieutenant Colonel Frank Jackson, which was the name I was known by at S.H.A.E.F., spread rapidly among my British Security circles and was no doubt being relayed to the enemy. There could be few to mourn his "death," I realized. "Frank Jackson" had not had the time or the opportunity to make many friends in his job. There would no doubt be many more—on the enemy side—for whom the news would be a matter of rejoicing. In the luxury of my peaceful resting I could hardly blame them.

By the end of March, 1945, I was completely recovered in health and strength and returned to duty on the Continent. Not six weeks later came V-E Day and with it the entire liberation of the northern provinces of Holland where pockets of German troops had still been resisting fanatically. My duties took me to The Hague early in June and one of my first tasks was to interrogate an S.S. man who was not a German but a Dutch collaborator.

He was held in the political prison nicknamed "The Orange Hotel" at the popular seaside resort, Scheveningen, near The Hague. The Canadian military authorities ran the prison, of which a special wing was reserved for my political prisoners and suspected spies or collaborators.

This particular prisoner had been "put in the bag" so

138

abruptly by the Dutch Resistance that he was still wearing the full-dress black S.S. uniform. A strip of red and black ribbon on the tunic denoted that he was the (no doubt) proud possessor of an Iron Cross. As I gazed at his bristling, cropped skull, his little piggy eyes and his arrogant bearing, which made him seem an exaggeration, a caricature of the qualities for which the S.S. were notorious, I thought to myself that this could only be an open-and-shut case. No man caught so red-handed in the full regalia of the enemy could find a plausible excuse. But I was wrong.

We went straight to the point in the cross-examination. "So you're a collaborator," I said. "It's going to be rather difficult for you to explain away this smart uniform, isn't it?"

He bristled with righteous indignation. "How dare you accuse me of being a collaborator? I am a good Dutchman who has done well by his country."

I stared at him. "You—a good Dutchman? By the same token, I suppose that Goering is the thinnest man alive and Himmler a Sunday School teacher. If you're such a great patriot how comes it that you were arrested in that uniform? And did the Germans honor you with their Iron Cross for being a good Dutchman? It's a strange world but this is beyond my powers of belief."

"You've got it all wrong, sir," he replied. "I admit it looks odd for a Dutchman to be seen in this rig-out but I can explain everything." He was working himself up into a rage. "It's a crying injustice for a man who has risked his life time and again for his country to be flung without

139

warning into this prison when all the real collaborators and friends of the dirty Hun are rolling around at liberty and even being made a fuss of. Now the Germans are kicked out, they've all crept out of their holes and dropped into the cushy jobs. To see them rolling around in their cars and living off the fat of the land you'd never think they'd been hand in glove with the enemy. And here am I, an honest man, who's done a tough job, rotting in prison. It's not fair."

I let his tirade run down. "Well, tough man," I said, "tell me some more. This is intriguing."

"Oh, I can see you don't believe me, sir, but it's the truth. I swear it. I joined the S.S. because I was ordered to do so. By a high-up officer in the Secret Service. He gave me very definite instructions, how I was to enroll, what I was to reply to their questions and so forth. And once I'd enlisted he told me what to look out for and what facts to discover. He even arranged for me to report once a month to one of his liaison officers. I was to meet this fellow in Rotterdam. At the quayside, the Boompjes, they call it."

I did not believe this story for I had heard too many variations on it in the course of many years. It struck me, however, that a court-martial might possibly uphold it, unless definite proof to the contrary could be obtained. There were indeed many genuine cases where agents had been infiltrated into the enemy forces and such men not only risked their lives daily but at the end of hostilities ran the added risk of being accused and sentenced as col-

140

laborators with the enemy. It was just possible that this present man was genuine but I did not think so. In any case, a decision had to be made one way or the other, so the cross-examination went on.

"All right," I said. "You had to meet this liaison officer once a month at Rotterdam and pass on any useful information you picked up. What was his name, so that I can have it checked in our records?"

The prisoner smiled in a superior way. "In Secret Service work, sir, a man does not go around asking for names and addresses. The less you know about a man personally the less there is to give away. I never asked him his name and never told him mine. We had too much important business to transact to waste time swapping our cards."

"I see. Thank you for giving me that tip on Secret Service work. It may come in useful. Since you cannot tell me the name of this anonymous liaison officer, is there anything more you can tell me about him?"

He thought for a moment. "Well, sir, I met him, as I told you, through the instructions of this high-up in the Secret Service."

"Ah yes," I said, "now we're getting somewhere. This high-up—you must surely have known something more definite about him, his name and so forth. You've only got to tell me his name and I can get him to confirm your story. If he does so, you'll be out of here like a shot."

The prisoner shook his head and looked sorrowful. "That's just the point, sir. If my old friend were available, I wouldn't still be rotting in this cell. He'd have got me

141

released ages go. But the unfortunate thing is—he's dead."

"Dead! Did the Gestapo get him?"

"Not him, sir! The Gestapo could never catch him—he's far too slippery for them. No, he died a natural death, poor chap."

"What was the matter with him?"

"I did hear it was cancer, sir—a cancer in the stomach."

I had a strange sensation in my own stomach at that moment. I went on, "Well, that's a great pity but never mind. Even if he's dead he may still be able to help you. If you can tell me his name, I can make inquiries and probably there'll be some mention of you in his Top Secret documents, or one of his assistants may be able to know about your case. Now, what's his name?"

The answer came without hesitation. "Jackson, sir. Lieutenant Colonel Frank Jackson."

It was difficult for me to keep a straight face. I found it necessary to sneeze abruptly and take my time over wiping my nose.

"Yes, I think I've heard of him," I said. "But I didn't know he had died. Still, when you're moving around a great deal, you miss a lot of news. Anyway, let's go on. It was this Colonel Frank Jackson who gave you detailed orders to join the S.S., was it?"

"Yes, sir."

"Had you known him for long?"

"Oh yes, sir. For years. Many's the job I've done for him."

"So Colonel Jackson trusted you implicitly, did he?"

142

"Oh, indeed, sir. He knew I'd do anything for him—risk my life if he gave the word. And he'd do anything for me, sir. If he were still alive, he'd have got me out of this long before now."

"I don't think you've much to worry about, even if he's dead. I shall have to make the usual inquiries but it seems a straightforward case, and somewhere in Colonel Jackson's headquarters we ought to come across the man or the documents that will clear you. As a matter of interest, because although I've heard a good deal about Colonel Jackson I never actually met him face to face, can you describe him to me?"

The prisoner screwed up his face in concentration. "I am not much good at describing people's looks and besides there wasn't anything remarkable about his appearance." The man's face lit up with a lucky inspiration. "I think that was part of his success, sir. He got by so well in Secret Service work just because he wouldn't stand out in a crowd. On the whole, he was pretty average to look at, average height and build, no peculiarities I can recall."

"I see. Would you say he was anything like me to look at, for instance?"

The prisoner looked at me and then laughed. "Good God, no! He wasn't a bit like you, sir."

"That's all right then," I said. "Well, your case seems pretty straightforward and I'm glad to have had this chat with you. As soon as I've had the chance of checking your story with the records, I'll make sure you're moved on

143

from here. And seeing what you've done for your country, I'll make it my business to see you get what you deserve."

"Oh, thank you very much, sir. I can't tell you how much I appreciate your kindness."

"Think nothing of it. I'd do as much for any man in your position. By the way, you could do one thing for me."

"What's that, sir?" He was eager to please.

"After I've gone, you'll probably remember all sorts of details about the secret work you've done. They might come in very useful and in any case I'd be interested to know the details of your dangerous job. At your leisure you could jot down all your memoirs of what you've done these past few years and don't leave out anything, however insignificant it might seem. I'll arrange with the warden for you to have all the writing material you require. When you've finished your notes, I'd like you to hand them over to the warden and if they're properly addressed to me, he can forward them on."

"Very good, sir. I'll do my best." As an afterthought he added, "By the way, sir, who shall I address the notes to? I'm afraid I don't know your name."

I said nothing for a moment and just stared at him. "My name? In this job I'm known as Jackson—Lieutenant Colonel Frank Jackson!"

Note: I still carry the military specialist's diagnosis in my wallet, partly as a souvenir and partly to remind myself that even experts can occasionally make errors. O. P.

144

CHAPTER IX

He Talked in the End

As has already been pointed out, it is always dangerous for a Counter-Intelligence officer to trust to his impressions of suspects. The expert spy will be trained to create
a good impression; part of his stock in trade may be his
open, honest-seeming countenance and his air of frankness.
He is out to establish the idea that he is a genuine and
decent citizen and, if he is anything of an actor, his ability
will be diverted to that end. A really honest and innocent
man, on the other hand, will not be practiced at creating
good impressions, unless he happens to be a salesman or
commercial traveler in private life where the ability to express a pleasant personality is important. Further, the innocent man has not the same pressing need to establish his
integrity under a cross-examination. He *knows* that he is
innocent and expects his interrogators to realize the fact
without assistance from him.

It is therefore unwise to jump to conclusions at first
sight in Counter-Intelligence work. Nevertheless, the man
with great experience can often make an immediate summing up which may appear intuitive but which is in fact
based on certain signs that appear to him at once although
they would probably be missed by the untrained observer.

145

Just as an architect can sum up a set of plans, or at least gain a definite impression of them, at a glance, or an editor assess an article by skimming over it quickly, so also can a trained interrogator derive important information from his first glimpses of a suspect. It is unwise to follow hunches blindly, but all the same hunches often lead one to the demonstrable truths.

I cannot now recall which sense or combination of senses warned me that Emile Boulanger may have been a German spy. The break-through had begun and the Allied spearheads were driving into Belgium. The tanks and motorized infantry were thrusting ahead and the restless thunder of the guns was just beyond the skyline. Near a road and lane junction we had set up a temporary Intelligence Headquarters, a thing of slit trenches and dugouts with their walls shored up by sandbags. The neighboring farm buildings and outhouses had been taken over by Divisional Headquarters. As comparative interlopers, my small unit had to fend for itself. (There were advantages in being attached rather loosely to a senior headquarters. We could come and go and be our own masters for the most part. But there were disadvantages as well. Nobody was responsible for our welfare, so when it came to finding accommodation we had to fend for ourselves as best we could.)

To return to Emile Boulanger. He was brought to my command post by two Field Security soldiers from the Divisional staff. They had found him wandering about in a dazed condition near an evacuated Belgian village where blackened stumps of walls and mounds of stone rubble

146

were the mute results of concentrated shelling. I looked at Boulanger for a long time without speaking. He was dressed as a typical farmer and the few words I had heard him utter were spoken in the Belgian-French and with the true accent of the Walloon countryman. But something in his bearing and in the bright glitter of his blue eyes made me suspicious. He was bull-necked and his muscular control differed from the shambling posture of the ordinary peasant in that part of the country.

"You are a farmer?" I asked.

"I was a farmer," he replied. He gestured with limp hands. "Now I have no farm. The Boche took my animals— even my little ducks. My fields are covered in shell holes, my cottage is in bits. My wife lies there dead—under the smashed roof. The others have gone—vanished."

Suddenly he held out his hands. He bent his fingers like claws. I could see that the fingernails were cracked and seamed with dirt. The finger tips were scratched and raw. Dried blood was caked in the crevices of the nails.

"I dug for her—my wife," he muttered in a half whisper. "She was under the ruins in the darkness and she was always afraid of the dark. I scratched like a hen—but she was dead." He lapsed into a brooding silence.

"Can you count?" I asked, breaking into his reverie.

"Count?" He blinked at the odd question.

There happened to be a dish of dried beans at hand, "liberated" by our troops from some thrifty peasant. I pushed the dish toward him. "Count these," I said, "aloud."

He picked up each bean slowly and in a wondering voice

147

began in French, "Un—deux—trois—" When he reached seventy-two I stopped him. He had passed one test successfully. If he had been a German linguist masquerading as a Walloon Belgian, he would probably have said the orthodox French for seventy-two: *soixante-douze*, and would not have known that Walloon farmers always say *septante-deux* for seventy-two. So far, so good. But I was still not satisfied that Boulanger was really what he purported to be—an honest Belgian farmer, dazed with grief at the loss of his house and his wife. Fortunately there was something of a lull in my activities at that time and I was able to devote more attention to him than I would normally have been able to. If he were proved innocent, no one would lose anything by it. If he were found guilty, we should have done a good job in maintaining the security behind the advancing forward troops.

I ordered him to be put in a small room by himself. It was part of a disused cowshed. The door was barred on the outside and there was a crack between two beams which acted as a natural spy hole. Through this crack he was kept under constant watch. Before going to bed that night, Boulanger knelt down to say his prayers. He could not have known that keen eyes were watching his every movement yet he said his prayers in Belgian in the simple, homely phrases that a Walloon village priest might have taught him as a child. A rat scurried across the bare floor. Startled, he said *"Dieu!"* a typical Walloon ejaculation. He stretched out on his mattress and seemed to drop asleep.

A little while later I arranged for some straw to be

148

placed against the outside of his door and lit. As the acrid smoke curled under the door, several soldiers ran clattering down the flagged corridor, shouting *"Feuer, feuer!"* the German for "Fire!" Boulanger stirred, appeared to wake up momentarily and then rolled over on his side again. A few moments later the soldiers ran down the corridor once more, shouting *"Au feu, au feu!"* the French for "Fire!" Boulanger sprang at once from his mattress and, screaming in fear, pounded on the heavily barred door. When I opened it, he was sobbing prayers in Belgian-French.

He had passed yet another test but I was still not satisfied. Was he genuine or was he a German spy with an excellent nerve and much acting ability? It was still not possible to say, although admittedly I seemed to have fewer grounds for doubting him.

Next morning I decided to try another way of testing him. I arranged for him to be brought to my field headquarters and a short while before he was due to arrive, told my plan to one of my junior officers who was to be present at the interview. After I had asked Boulanger several questions, I would mutter, *"Armer Kerl,"* which means "Poor chap" in German. The officer was to reply, *"Warum?"* ("Why?") and then he was to let me go on speaking in German.

Boulanger was escorted in. On the folding camp table behind which I sat were spread the few possessions we found on him at the time of his arrest. They were ordinary enough. There was the stub of a pencil, a bit of string, a

149

sodden lump of partly chewed tobacco, a clumsy, home-made crucifix and a few francs. There seemed to be nothing very sinister in this pathetic collection of odds and ends.

Boulanger stood there, patient and sullen like an animal in its stall. I turned over his few belongings and then picked up the pencil. "Why did you carry this on you?" I asked, in French.

"It is only a pencil," he said, shrugging his strong, heavy shoulders.

"Did you carry it so that you could write messages to the enemy?" He smiled vaguely and looked at me almost with contempt, as though the question were too foolish to require answering.

I turned to the security officer and said in German as arranged, "Poor chap."

He took up the cue promptly. "Why?" he asked in the same language.

Still speaking German, I went on, "Because he does not realize that he will be hanged within an hour from now. It is after eleven o'clock," I glanced at my watch, "and I have ordered his execution for noon. He is obviously a spy and cannot expect a better fate."

All the time I was speaking I watched Boulanger keenly, especially his eyes and his Adam's apple. However brave and self-controlled a man may be, he usually has little control over what are technically called the vasomotor nerves which react automatically. Just as a man will blink unconsciously if an object suddenly approaches his eyes, so also will a man who hears of his impending death be liable to go pale, or blink in astonishment or swallow as his mouth grows unbearably dry. But Boulanger did none of these things. Although he must have known himself to be under suspicion as a spy, he stood there stolidly without moving or showing the least signs of alarm. The obvious deduction was that he had not understood the language I had used and could not therefore be a German spy.

By this stage I had to admit to myself that my original swift summing up, based as it was on intangible evidence, appeared to be very wide of the mark. Perhaps it was stubbornness on my part or the dislike of seeing my vanity wounded by admitting I had made a mistake or even the prompting of my subconscious instincts. Whatever the reason, I decided to test Boulanger again.

Next day I arranged for a loyal Belgian countryman to meet my suspect. I was present at their meeting. When at my prompting the countryman began to talk of farming, Boulanger for the first time became animated and broke eagerly into the discussion. Even to my nonexpert eye he seemed to know a great deal about local farming and the countryman told me afterward that he had not made a single mistake over crops or local conditions and methods.

Once again I had to admit reaching a dead end in my tests. The suspicion was growing with each rebuff that I had made a big mistake in suspecting him in the first place. After advising all the beginners who had ever learned Counter-Intelligence methods from me that one should never allow first impressions to sway one's judgment, here was I falling into that very trap with all the clumsy haste

151

of the rank amateur. I sat long in the night trying to analyze the feelings that had made me suspicious of Boulanger at first sight. Then I mentally ran through his actions and words from that moment to this, trying to find some hint or clue that would endorse my earlier judgment. Rack my memory as I might, I could not find the elusive point that would have reinforced my suspicions. Finally, before turning in for the night, I decided to try one last test on him in the morning. If it failed, I was prepared to admit freely that I had unjustly suspected him of being a spy and would have him released on the spot. I was even prepared to make him a handsome apology for having doubted him.

He came into my office next morning and stood there, just as stolid and patient as ever. My head was lowered as I read a typed document on my desk. Reaching the end, I took up a pen and signed at the foot of the page. Laying down the pen, I looked up and said sharply, *"So, jetzt bin ich zufrieden. Sie können gehen. Sie sind frei."* ("All right, I am now satisfied. You can go. You are free.")

He breathed a deep sigh of relief, shook his shoulders as though a heavy weight had fallen from them and lifted his face happily to gulp in the air of freedom. When he heard my chuckle, he stiffened and tried to relapse into his previous resigned posture but it was too late. At a quick signal the hands of his escorts were already gripping his shoulders.

"Mein lieber Freund," I said and stood up. From then until his execution a few days later we spoke nothing but his native German.

152

CHAPTER X

The Traitor of Arnhem

1

THE case I am now going to relate is certainly the most important that I ever experienced and is perhaps one of the most important spy cases in the whole history of espionage.

Let us consider the facts. If Field Marshal Montgomery's daring bid for a spearhead attack across the Maas and Neder Rijn bridgeheads had succeeded and had the main forces linked up with the gallant paratroopers at Arnhem, a wedge of armor would have been thrust at the heart of Germany. Successful exploitation of the thrust would probably have ended the war in Europe before Christmas, 1944, six months sooner than was in fact the case. It is impossible to measure the saving in the lives of soldiers and civilians which would have resulted from such a shortening of the war. Hundreds of millions of pounds' worth of devastation of land and buildings would have been avoided. The British Government alone was spending some £16,000,000 per day in the war effort at that time. Had the European war been shortened by six months, it would have saved a

153

gigantic sum in the neighborhood of £2,900,000,000 for the Exchequer. When one considers what other governments, notably the United States, were jointly spending in prosecuting the war, the monies that might have been saved and later devoted to reconstruction for peace would amount to astronomical figures. More important still, had the Western Allies penetrated far into Germany and occupied all of Berlin and West Germany before the Russians had arrived from the east, the whole sad story of Allied relations since 1945 might have been far different.

There are good grounds for claiming that the parachute landings at Arnhem, so boldly planned and daringly executed, might have been the turning point of the European war if they had succeeded. They did not succeed, as the whole world knows, but not for want of military skill and courage. In fact Arnhem is a bright flower of the British ability to fight on to the end against overwhelming odds. One man—and one man only—made the Arnhem landings a doomed venture from the start. He was a Dutchman named Christian Lindemans. Whether or not we can blame him for causing a six months' prolongation of the European war with all its attendant sacrifices and tragedies, we can certainly charge him with the 7,000 casualties suffered by the gallant airborne forces during the ten days in which the trap they had dropped into slowly closed its jaws on them. Few spies turned traitors could claim responsibility for dealing such damage at one blow to their country's cause.

154

2

My job as head of the Netherlands Counter-Intelligence Mission attached to S.H.A.E.F. gave me the responsibility of organizing in the area allotted to me the security arrangements behind the armies advancing through Flanders into Holland. This group of armies consisted of the British Second Army, the United States First and Third Armies and the Canadian First Army, a massive body of men and machines. As the tanks, the self-propelled guns and the infantry rolled forward, inevitably they left a trail of devastation and ruin behind them. Inevitably, many of the unfortunate civilians who lived in the path of the advancing armies were rendered homeless by shelling and bombing, particularly in those areas where the retreating Germans fought savage rearguard actions. Civil control was almost nonexistent, since many members of the police forces and local authorities who had acted during the German occupation were either discredited or in hiding. Looting, famine, revolt were the grisly camp followers of the war. The Germans had not been slow to exploit these circumstances and had left behind them spies and saboteurs to continue the war from the rear of the Allied lines. Everything was in confusion and many civilians were making the most of their opportunity to pay off old scores and to indulge their wants free from police control.

Law and order had to be established promptly. Nothing would have pleased the German forces more than to cause Allied front-line troops to be taken out of the line for the task of restoring security in the rear areas. The methods we

155

adopted therefore were rough and ready but at least effective. Big camps were set up by taking an open space and enclosing it in a solid ring of barbed wire. Machine guns were erected around the perimeter and sighted to fire both inward and outward. Guards patrolled the wire and the one or two gates allowing entry or exit were manned continuously by sentries. All the homeless, the refugees, the suspected collaborators and spies were put into these camps and then gradually sorted out. As soon as the honest citizens could establish their innocence they were removed to more congenial quarters. Gradually through this constant filtering only the "dregs" were left and they were interrogated, tried and punished according to their deserts. The method involved depriving the innocent of their liberty for several days, but in war unfortunately the guiltless often have to suffer for the good of the greater cause. We could not afford to make mistakes that might have seriously impeded the advance of the Allied Armies.

After Antwerp had been liberated, I had arranged for one of these large security camps to be erected in the neighborhood. I happened to be passing near the main gate one day when I heard a commotion and went over to see what was happening. It was a surprising sight. Towering over the sentry on duty was a giant of a man. Well over six feet in height he was disproportionately broad, with a massive chest that strained and threatened to split his khaki shirt. His biceps bulging against the sleeves of his jacket seemed to be as big as an athlete's thigh. He must have weighed nearly eighteen stone but he was hard and solid

156

all over, like a great monolith of a man. As if his physical appearance were not enough to make him stand out from the crowd, he was like a miniature mobile arsenal in the weapons he carried. In his leather belt were stuck two dark steel killing knives. A long-barreled Luger pistol with marksman's sights graduated to one thousand meters was strapped to his right hip. A Schmeisser submachine gun was slung across his huge chest and looked almost as innocuous as a water pistol in contrast. His pockets had a sinister bulge that to my eye spelled out the presence of hand grenades.

This giant apparition had a smiling girl on each arm and was surrounded by a gaggle of admiring Dutch youths, obviously hero-worshiping him. The sentry who was barring his way was embarrassed and hesitant. As I approached the group from behind, I heard the giant rumble in a deep voice, "Ach, these two girls are good Dutch patriots. Tell your Colonel that the great King Kong has vouched for them. They are to be released at once to drink wine with me."

I had of course heard of this "King Kong," the daring leader of the Dutch resistance forces who had been given the nickname for obvious reasons. His was a revered name in Occupied Europe for his brute strength, his fearlessness and the brilliant coups he had engineered against the Germans. But he had no right to come swaggering into the camp, to pick up a couple of girls and remove them before they had been screened by the proper authorities. Let him by all means be a hero in his own sphere but here he was trespassing.

157

I shouted out to him, "Come here—you."

He turned round, blinked and shrugged off the girls. He tapped his mighty chest with a forefinger that seemed to be as thick as my wrist. "Were you talking to me?"

"Yes, you. Come here."

He hesitated and then swaggered over to me, towering inches above me although I am of average height. Before he had a chance to speak I touched the three gold stars he wore on his sleeve.

"By what right do you wear those? Are you a captain and, if so, in what army?"

He expelled his breath in a growl. "Now see here, I wear these three stars by authority of the Dutch Interior Forces—the Underground!"

"Really? And who are you?" I asked with mock naïveté.

"Me?" He was astounded that anyone could be so ignorant. He turned round to his loyal supporters and shrugged in dumb show as if to say that here was the eighth wonder of the world—a man who could not recognize the great "King Kong" at first sight. "Who am I? Why, Colonel, everyone knows who I am." His voice bellowed out. "I live at Castle Wittouck, headquarters of the Dutch resistance." He paused and swelled his mighty chest until I expected the buttons to burst off his shirt. "I—I am King Kong!"

"The only King Kong I ever heard of," I replied softly, "was a big stuffed monkey."

There was a titter from the sycophants behind him. He clenched his teeth and his fists so that for a moment he did

158

actually resemble his cinematic namesake. My hand slid unobtrusively toward the Walthur automatic pistol I always carried in my shoulder holster. If he managed to grasp me in those gigantic fists I realized he could break me in two as easily as one snaps a dry stick. But he merely glowered at me without making a move.

Sensing my advantage, I pressed on. "As you do not hold the rank of captain in the Netherlands Army, you are not entitled to wear the insignia," I said. I reached out and ripped off the cloth band with the three gold stars which he wore on his sleeve.

His Neanderthal jaw sagged and he changed color. By now my hand was hovering over the pistol butt in case he attacked me in a sudden frenzy of wounded pride. But he stepped backward instead of forward. For a second the great King Kong looked sheepish, like a truant schoolboy. Then mustering his self-respect he shouted, "I shall make a formal complaint of your treatment at Castle Wittouck without delay." He strode away, leaving the two girls and his crowd of admirers gaping at his sudden departure.

3

So that was my first meeting with King Kong. In the ordinary way I should have been glad to greet him and pay my respects to the great resistance leader, the "Scarlet Pimpernel" of Holland who had saved from the Gestapo dozens of refugees and Allied airmen shot down over Occupied Holland by conducting them along the secret escape routes, who had fought daring skirmishes with the

159

Nazi Sicherheitsdienst, the dreaded S.D. Security Police, and who had thumbed his nose at their efforts to trap him. Had he followed the formal courtesies of applying for permission to enter the camp, I should have welcomed him warmly and would have opened a bottle of wine in his honor at the mess. But as chief security officer of the camp, I was not prepared to have my authority flouted and a bad example given to the inmates and guards by allowing a civilian, however well-earned his fame, to break all the rules of military etiquette and ride roughshod over the regulations.

Musing on the encounter afterward, I wondered whether I had perhaps treated my unexpected visitor too summarily. To deflate his arrogance so publicly might be an unwarranted piece of overofficiousness. He had behaved badly in the first place but possibly through sheer ignorance of military custom. Had I perhaps acted equally badly, if not worse, in treating him with undue severity?

And then a strange idea occurred to me, one of those flashes of intuition which often produce an unexpected train of thought. Why had he submitted so meekly to my brusque treatment? Any man with his outstanding record, even when consciously in the wrong, should surely have stood his ground and defended himself, especially when surrounded by hero-worshipers. Yet King Kong had suffered public humiliation without any more effective reply than a blustering threat and had retreated hastily at the earliest opportunity. Such conduct did not seem typical of the man and his reputation. Perhaps it needed investigating.

On my return to Intelligence Headquarters at S.H.A.E.F., I sent for my assistant. He was a remarkable fellow whose varied career had included being a sergeant in the French Foreign Legion and also a spy in Tangiers. He possessed an encyclopedic memory which was the repository of odd facts and bits of information about the underground movements throughout Europe and the spies who worked on both sides of the "fence."

"Tell me, Wilhelm," I asked, "what do we know about the resistance leader nicknamed King Kong?"

He paused for a moment, screwed up his face in concentration and then rattled off the facts. "Real name Christian Lindemans. Born in Rotterdam, the son of a garage owner. Ex-boxer and wrestler. Reported to have killed several men in tavern brawls. Dozens of girls listed as his intimate friends." He grinned slyly. "Would you like their names?"

I shook my head. "Anything else?"

"Yes, sir. He's the eldest of four brothers—all resistance men working on the escape line."

"Any been killed?" I asked.

Wilhelm's memory failed him for a moment. He went over to a filing cabinet and, riffling through the files, selected one. He turned over the sheets and then paused. "No, none of them have been killed. One, the youngest brother, was captured by the Abwehr and so was a cabaret dancer named Veronica, shown here as intimate with Lindemans. They were both working on the escape line."

161

He ran a finger down the typed page. "Both were later released."

"They were *what?*"

He shrugged his shoulders. "That's what it says here—they were both released. Seems odd for the German Intelligence to release its prisoners, doesn't it?—but that's what the report says."

"Anything else?" I asked. The tension in me was growing, and suspicions, from being a vague uneasiness, were beginning to crystallize.

"Yes, sir. Lindemans himself was captured by the Gestapo in a raid a few weeks later. He was shot through the lung, I see. His own resistance group rescued him from a prison hospital after a running gunfight."

"Many killed?"

"Yes—one S.S. guard killed, two wounded. The resistance men came off worse, though. Lindemans got away with three of them but the other forty-seven were all killed. Ambushed as they withdrew from the hospital."

"Almost as if the Germans had known beforehand," I said slowly.

Wilhelm stared at me, his eyes narrowed. He could guess the ideas passing through my mind. Then he nodded but said nothing.

"I'll borrow that dossier for two or three days," I said, reaching out for the file that lay on the table between us. "With any luck I may be able to add a page or two to it. I'll leave for Brussels in the morning."

162

4

Once in Brussels, I found the problem was not so much locating men and women who had known Lindemans intimately but fobbing off the dozens who claimed intimate knowledge of him. A national hero in his native Holland, he was also a popular figure in Belgium and there were many who wished to bask in his reflected glory by posing as his closest friend. I could fill the pages of another book with the various stories, some with a germ of truth but mostly the wildest fiction, of his exploits which were told me by those who claimed his acquaintance. I was not looking for people who had once passed the time of day with King Kong and thereafter looked on themselves as his most trusted comrades in arms. I wanted men who had actually worked in the resistance with him and who could build up or refute the theory that was forming in my mind.

After a while I came on the track of one such man and arranged an appointment with him in the Café des Vedettes. We chatted amiably and before long I realized from his remarks that he really did know Lindemans and had worked with him.

"Were you one of the lucky ones who got away from that hospital raid?" I asked.

"No, unfortunately I missed that party. I got this little *souvenir de la guerre* about a month afterward." He pulled off his greasy black beret and proudly pointed to a bullet scar that ploughed a neat furrow across his scalp.

"A near thing," I remarked.

He grinned. "Yes, sir, quite close enough for my health's

163

sake. I would have been most upset if it had arrived an inch or so lower."

"How did it happen?"

"Well, sir, we were dynamiting a bridge. I was just bending down, fixing the fuses to the charges under the bridge stanchion when—just like that"—he snapped his fingers quickly once, twice, thrice—"bullets began to crack all over the place. Somehow the Nazis had got wind of our plan and had planted an ambush. The sudden shock knocked me off the bridge into the river and luckily I had the presence of mind to stay under water until the current—it was very fast just there—pulled me out of sight of their guns. King Kong, our leader—he was magnificent! He got away right from under their noses. But the others—" He shrugged his shoulders.

"What were they shooting with?" I asked. "Machine guns?"

The honest little Belgian patriot replaced his dirty black beret. "Strangely enough, they weren't. You'd have expected machine guns on a job like that but the odd thing was they all had sniper's rifles. They picked us off one after the other, like knocking tins off a wall. Every man hit—and there were eight of us—except King Kong. They couldn't hit him. What a man! He was born lucky, that one!"

"Strange," I said quietly. "The biggest target of all—and they couldn't hit him."

"*Oui-dà!* Such a big target. But he was too smart for them was our great King Kong!"

164

A picture of sorts was beginning to take shape in my mind. Here was the famous resistance leader on the one hand, the man whose daring, giant strength and romantic affairs had made him the darling of all patriotic Dutchmen and almost equally popular with his Belgian comrades. A born leader who had done the Nazis much damage and who had risked his life repeatedly for his country. On the debit side were four strange facts which did not yet add up to any conclusion. He had been strangely apprehensive when I had tackled him over wearing insignia of rank to which he was not entitled. He had not then behaved like an honest man who had nothing to fear. The Gestapo had released his brother and girl friend from captivity. It was not like the Gestapo to lose the opportunity of revenging themselves, even indirectly, on one of their most hated enemies. The third and the fourth facts were that on at least two separate occasions, someone had obviously betrayed a resistance raid to the Gestapo sufficiently far in advance for them to plant a careful ambush. In each case the only common factor who had escaped was the leader—King Kong. The evidence was by no means decisive but it was growing beyond the stage of coincidence.

I poured out some more red wine for the little resistance man. "They say that King Kong has an eye for the ladies," I remarked casually.

"Oh yes, sir, there they speak the truth! He is *très galant*—not a girl who would not give anything to feel those big arms around her. I tell you, the pretty heiress who lives in the big château on the hill beyond Laeken—

165

they say she gave all her jewelry, her family heirlooms, for his resistance group war funds." He smiled tolerantly. "They also say he gave the sparklers away to other girls here in Brussels. But it is all rumors, rumors, where King Kong is concerned. There never was a great man who didn't have some dirty rumors spread about him by the envious."

Shortly afterward the interview ended. I drove off at once to the château near Laeken and found the lady of the castle at home. After the preliminary courtesies we began to discuss Lindemans. Yes, she had given him her family jewels but she was careful to stress that she had done so out of patriotic regard for the resistance movement. He was a great man, indeed, but he had his weaknesses. She suspected that he had embezzled the jewels and not sold them for resistance funds.

"What makes you think that, Countess?" I asked.

"I do not like saying so, because after all he is such a brave man and has done such fine things for Belgium. But one day I saw a girl in the town wearing one of my emerald pendants. She was not a respectable girl, you understand? The pendant had belonged to my mother and I did not think it suitable that a girl of this kind should wear it. I thought that perhaps the resistance men had sold it locally to raise money, so I asked the girl if she would sell it to me, without telling her that it had once been mine. She said King Kong had given it to her and would strangle her if she sold it."

"Did you find out her name?"

The Countess sighed. "Ah, if there had only been the one girl. No, there were two—Mia Zeist was one and the other was called—let me see—ah, yes, Margaretha Delden. They were both notorious tavern girls here."

Fortunately she did not glance up as she spoke for she would have seen a strange look on my face. Mia Zeist and Margaretha Delden were both listed on my security files as paid and highly valuable agents of the German Abwehr!

Terminating the interview as soon as I could without disturbing the conventions, I drove back to Brussels as fast as the camouflaged staff car would take me. There I put a telephone call through to Intelligence Headquarters at Antwerp. After some delay Wilhelm, my assistant, was brought to the telephone. Had he the addresses of Mia Zeist and Margaretha Delden? Yes, he could produce them, and after a few minutes did so. I borrowed a couple of security policemen from the Dutch Intelligence in Brussels and together we rushed to the first address.

We were too late. The flat was empty. Mia Zeist had fled—we learned later—to Vienna.

Jumping into the staff car, we drove to Margaretha Delden's apartment. The door was heavily bolted. We had no search warrant but there was no time to observe the niceties of etiquette. We smashed the door in. We burst into her room and found her lying on the bed. Normally she must have been a pretty girl but poison does not improve one's features. Her face was a mottled color, like those marbled end papers one sometimes comes across in old books and ledgers. Her lips were a ghastly magenta

167

in color and were stretched in a mirthless grin. She was still just breathing when we found her but she died in hospital that afternoon, without uttering a word.

So two vital witnesses in what I was already calling mentally the "Lindemans Case" were to be written off the list. One had wisely fled in time. The other had killed herself and in dying had been faithful to the end to Lindemans, although to him she had only been one of many. We recovered the Countess's emerald pendant but that was poor consolation.

I spent a further day and a night in Brussels, combing the back streets, the sordid cafés and the smoky cellars for more details of Lindemans' career. Gradually the jigsaw was being pieced together. Several independent witnesses confirmed that when his younger brother had been captured by the Abwehr Lindemans was deeply in debt. In spite of his popularity various tradesmen and private citizens to whom he owed comparatively large sums were threatening to foreclose on him. I also learned that the cabaret dancer Veronica, who had been captured at the same time as the younger brother, had been King Kong's sweetheart from childhood. In spite of his countless amours and intrigues she had always been constant to him and he had always in the end come back to her. The Nazis must have known this and yet they had released both her and the younger brother without so much as breaking a leg or two or tearing out the odd fingernail as a memento of their enforced visit. It was not like the Nazis to show such clemency.

168

Other witnesses confirmed that, coinciding with the release of his sweetheart and his brother, Lindemans became suddenly affluent. Not only did he pay off all his debts but he lived even more riotously and expensively. He also grew increasingly reckless in his guerrilla battles with the Nazis. Each raid was more daring than the last and each suffered heavier casualties. Always the heroic leader escaped by the skin of his teeth, blazing away with his arsenal of weapons and using his giant strength to save himself. He would swear blood-curdling threats of vengeance on the Judas who must have betrayed the raid in advance but strangely enough the traitor was never discovered. And tragically there was never a lack of volunteers to accompany the redoubtable King Kong on his forays. It was considered an honor to risk almost certain death at his side.

It seemed strange to me that no breath of suspicion tarnished King Kong's own reputation. All the survivors whose stories I listened to were loud in their praises of his daring and resourcefulness. Surely, I thought, it should sooner or later have struck someone as a strange coincidence that King Kong himself always escaped? On reflection I realized that the very extent of his reputation could be a formidable cloak for treacherous activities. This swaggering giant of a man with his gallantry and lavish ways would appear almost superhuman, an indestructible being, to the little unknown men—the real heroes—who themselves hero-worshiped him and went gaily to their deaths for a smile and a pat on the back from one of his huge hands. And there was always the inescapable fact that he had himself

169

been wounded, shot through the lung, and then captured by the German Security Police.

This idea made me pause. Was I being premature in condemning him as a spy, in spite of the evidence against him? Not even the fat Herr Strauch of the Nazi Intelligence in the Netherlands would thus risk the life of a valuable agent just to add circumstantial detail to the appearance of an arrest.

I pondered over this problem for several hours, chain-smoking one cigarette after another. It was the one piece that completely upset the jigsaw which I had painstakingly fitted together. On all other counts Lindemans was to be strongly suspected as a traitor. But this one inexplicable fact seemed to disprove his guilt. And then, accidentally, a possible explanation hit me. As was always my habit, I was mentally retesting all the links in the chain of evidence in the Lindemans Case to date. I had reached the point where the Countess had spoken about Mia Zeist and Margaretha Delden. To find out their addresses I had had to telephone all the way to Antwerp, although I was actually in Brussels, their home town. The local Field Security had not known their addresses. Dutch Intelligence Headquarters in Brussels had not known. But S.H.A.E.F. Intelligence had known. We were all on the same side, fighting for the same general cause, but we had not pooled our information. There were always those petty rivalries and jealousies, the urge to keep the "plums" of information to one's own headquarters, which tended to mar the co-operation between different services and differ-

170

ent countries, all ostensibly on the same side for the same purpose.

Human nature being fairly constant the world over, it was reasonable to assume that a similar rivalry might exist between the three different branches of the German Intelligence—the Gestapo (the Security Police of the S.S.), the Abwehr (the Counter-Intelligence Service) and the Sicherheitsdienst (the German Field Security Police). If, as I suspected, Lindemans was a traitor in the pay of the Abwehr, since both his notorious girl friends had belonged to it, the Gestapo and the S.D. Police might easily not have known this. Thinking of him only as one of the most redoubtable resistance leaders, and of all men he was least able to disguise his bulk and appearance, they would probably shoot him on sight, only afterward discovering that he was a valuable ally.

If this reasoning were true, what a blessing in disguise was this bullet wound to Lindemans! It was the perfect answer to anyone who might suspect that he was a traitor. And thanks to this ironic stroke of fortune he would have been able to go his way unscathed, betraying his comrades to sudden death, and condemning no one would know how many British and Belgian agents along the escape route out of Occupied Europe to the torments of the Gestapo.

I decided that the circumstantial evidence against Lindemans was sufficiently strong to warrant my cross-examining him in person. I sent a message to the headquarters of Dutch Intelligence at Castle Wittouck, where Lindemans was supposed to have reported me for my cavalier conduct in

171

ripping off his badges a few days before. Needless to say, he had not acted on his threat. Instead I mentioned that I wanted the opportunity of a talk with him although I was careful not to reveal the main purpose behind my wish. Lindemans had many friends in high places, as was natural for so famous a resistance leader, and I dared not risk the possibility of some casual remark or deliberate "tip" fore-warning him of my real purpose. So I merely left word that he was to report to me at eleven o'clock next morning at the Palace Hotel, Brussels, where S.H.A.E.F. officers were billeted.

The next morning I was punctual at the rendezvous. It was a warm, balmy morning in which only peace seemed possible in the sunshine. But the war itself was only a few miles away and everywhere, even in the lounge of this luxurious hotel, war had left its trademark. The military had moved in and businesslike folding tables and wooden chairs had replaced the luxurious armchairs where the social elite of Brussels had once gossiped over their coffee.

The chimes of eleven o'clock rang mellowly through the lounge but there was yet no sign of Lindemans. I was not perturbed. He could hardly avoid coming, since I had left specific instructions, but he could assert his native arrogance by arriving late. As I ran mentally through the questions to be asked, my right hand felt the rough com-fort of the serrated grip of my Walthur automatic pistol which was loose in its holster. The action was cocked and there was a round in the breach. A slight pressure and it was ready for action. Lindemans might not yet realize that

172

this was to be a life-or-death meeting for him but I did. Compared to his height and great strength, I was a little weakling and in unarmed combat would not have rated my life worth a minute once those massive hairy hands clamped down on me. But had not Damon Runyon, the scribe of Broadway, described the automatic pistol as "the old equalizer"? Having it close to my hand canceled out the physical difference between Lindemans and myself. I had some natural talent for shooting and hours of practice with my favorite Walthur had made me something of an expert. In any case, if King Kong objected too strongly to my questions, I could hardly miss the vast target he presented across the narrow width of a coffee table.

The minutes went by and still there was no sign of him. I had expected him to be perhaps ten minutes or quarter of an hour late, even half an hour if he wanted to gain some revenge for the humiliation he had suffered at the Antwerp Security Camp. But when it was after twelve o'clock and he had not arrived, I began to wonder whether I had perhaps misjudged his arrogance. Was he so confident in his reputation and the friendships he enjoyed with the politically powerful that he would deliberately disobey a specific order?

I had waited nearly two hours when I found the answer. Two young Dutch captains strode smartly into the lounge of the hotel. From their bandbox appearance and the bright armbands they wore, I knew them as staff captains from the Netherlands General Headquarters staff. They marched

173

over to my table and saluted in unison. One of them spoke. "You are waiting for Lindemans, sir?"

"I am. And have been for nearly two hours."

"We're sorry, sir, that you've been kept waiting. Lindemans cannot keep the appointment. He's had other orders."

"Other orders. Whose orders?" I was growing angry but did not want these glossy young men to know it.

They drew themselves up even more erect and a tone of reverence crept into the spokesman's voice, like the hushed tone that the faithful use when they speak of God. "Lindemans left this morning on a very special mission."

My throat contracted so that I could hardly speak. I had hoped that following our meeting that would not now take place, Lindemans' treacherous activities would be curtailed even if I did not at once prove his guilt. And now he had not only eluded me but was probably this very moment leading brave men of the resistance into a well-prepared trap.

"With the Interior Forces?" I asked.

The two staff captains hesitated and then assumed the importance that nearly all men show when they know a major secret of which their interrogator is ignorant. "No, sir. He has been attached to the Canadians for special intelligence duties, but we are not permitted to tell you what those are, sir."

(Later I learned what had happened. The Canadians required a really trustworthy local man who could secretly enter Eindhoven which was still in German hands and get in touch with the leader of the resistance in that area. The

174

messenger was to inform the resistance leader that large Allied parachute landings were to take place north of Eindhoven the following Sunday morning, September 17, and the resistance leader was to prepare and concentrate his men to aid the paratroops and exploit the initial German confusion. The Canadians applied to Dutch Headquarters who at once thought of Lindemans as the man for this special mission, little knowing that he might be a traitor and that I was on his track. One cannot blame them for not suspecting Lindemans, although it must be added that the facts about him, his reckless spending, his constant miraculous escapes from ambushes, had been known to them for months, and were so plain that it had only taken me a few days to collect them and tot them up. Sending Lindemans on such an errand was equivalent to broadcasting the news of the forthcoming Allied parachute landings on the B.B.C. news bulletins.)

But I did not know that the landings were about to take place. All I could then hope—a pious hope!—was that the special mission Lindemans was engaged on would not cost us too dear in casualties. All I could do was to carry out that last resort of those who have failed—to make out my official report and send it to S.H.A.E.F.

5

What happened three days later is too well known to the world to need more than the briefest of descriptions. At dawn on September 17 the largest airborne landing in the history of warfare took place. Nearly ten thousand men

175

of the British 1st Airborne Division were dropped at Arnhem, while twenty thousand American paratroops and three thousand Poles were dropped at Grave and Nijmegen. Their task was to secure and hold bridgeheads over the Maas Canal, the Waal River and the Neder Rijn while armored spearheads from the main forces plunged down the major road to join up with these outposts and force the water crossings in bulk. The operation under its code name "Operation Market-Garden" was like threading beads on to a necklace of armor and fire power. It was a daring plan and everything depended on the surprise effect to be obtained by dropping parachute troops well behind the enemy's front lines. If the Germans in the rear areas were taken entirely by surprise, it was estimated that several days must pass before they could regroup for an attack on the airborne bridgeheads. By this time the main forces would be well on their way and if the paratroops, reinforced with supplies of food and ammunition dropped by air, could hold out, a brilliant victory would result.

Everything seemed to be going according to plan. Air reconnaissance on the morning of September 16 showed that there was no abnormal German activity in the Arnhem area. But after dark that night the German Panzers rumbled quietly into position, taking up hull-down positions behind hedgerows and ditches around the vital dropping area. At dawn the paratroops dropped out of the gray sky but not to find the enemy surprised and confused. From the start it was obvious that something had gone wrong but at the time everyone thought that a lucky coincidence had caused the Germans to consolidate their armor and infantry in the one place where they were neither expected nor wanted.

Nine days later, nine days of gallant and hopeless fighting against an enemy that surrounded them on all sides, with food and ammunition running out and with their ring of defense drawn so tight that air-dropped supplies were more likely to land among the Germans than themselves, two thousand four hundred survivors of the heroic "Red Devils of Arnhem" struggled to safety back across the Waal River, leaving seven thousand casualties behind them. The daring coup had failed. Montgomery had suffered his first and only major defeat of the war. The war itself was to be continued for another eight months of killing and devastation. In the "Black Winter" of wrecked dikes and trampled harvests that was to follow, nearly two hundred thousand Dutch men and women were to die through flood and famine. But still no one apart from myself seemed to suspect the real cause behind the failure of the operation. It was "one of those things," "the luck of the game" and so on. I was already fairly certain in my own mind that Lindemans was a traitor. Later, learning some hints of what his secret mission for the Canadians had entailed, I was all the more convinced.

6

Meanwhile although I was very busy on other cases, I had not shelved the Lindemans Case. The report which I had sent up to S.H.A.E.F. had no doubt been neatly filed in a pigeonhole somewhere in that enormous headquarters.

177

The Intelligence Branch had many different problems to consider and this would only be one of them. In any case, most senior officers who had to rely for their information on what was reported to them on paper would be likely to dismiss my suspicions as being utterly fantastic. To accuse the famous resistance leader of one of our Allies of being a traitor was not only absurd but was really in doubtful taste. Such a charge could easily have serious political and diplomatic repercussions. No soldier likes to be mixed up in politics or diplomacy in the middle of the greatest war yet known to mankind. All his instincts would be on the side of shelving such a nasty problem, if he could be persuaded for one moment to believe in the gravity of the charges. So nothing further occurred. Whenever I met my opposite number in the British Counter-Intelligence attached to S.H.A.E.F., a brilliant man who has subsequently occupied some of the most important political positions in the land, I tackled him on the subject of Lindemans. He was always courteous but I could see that he was not impressed with my deductions. If such a clever man with direct experience of Counter-Intelligence work felt no confidence in my claims, it was all the less likely that the "chair-borne" officers in S.H.A.E.F. with many diverse problems of immediate urgency to overcome would follow up my suggestsions.

So for six weeks no results came from my efforts to have Lindemans arrested. Thus far there was no absolute evidence of his guilt but only circumstantial evidence supported by deductions. Then one evening the additional

178

proof arrived dramatically. The Allied advance had continued, although since the tragic failure of Arnhem the armies had had to fight for every foot of ground they gained. I was in Eindhoven, which had now been taken, and was just concluding an interrogation which had lasted for nearly three hours. I had by this time been denuded of my assistants and also of my personal transport. I was working alone and had to act as interrogator, judge and jailer where my suspect was concerned.

He was a young Dutchman named Cornelis Verloop. I had finally trapped him into admitting he was a spy. He was at his wits' end with fear.

I stood up and stretched myself, dusting cigarette ash off my uniform. He watched me closely.

"Am I to be shot?" he whispered. His throat was too dry to allow him to speak normally.

I shrugged without answering. It seemed obvious that he was going to be shot. He was a spy.

"I have a young wife in Amsterdam, sir, a good Dutch girl. She is innocent, I swear it."

"So? We do not propose to shoot your wife. We are not like your German masters."

Desperately he tried another tack. "I will give you valuable information, sir—in return for my life."

"You fool," I said. "Any information you have can be extracted from you before you are shot. It is a simple and painless process."

He gave a wan but sly smile. "You can make me tell

179

what you think I should know but you cannot find out those facts which you do not suspect I know."

"Well, my young philosopher, what do you know?" There was an edge of contempt to my tone.

Verloop leaned forward eagerly and, squeezing his fists together to aid his memory, recited the names and descriptions of all my Intelligence Headquarters staff. Even many G.H.Q. staff officers did not know the identities of some of the men whose names Verloop rattled off.

"Also, your chief agent in Brussels is Paul Leuven and in Amsterdam a man named Dampreny, and—" He sat there at the table and glibly recited the main network of our counterespionage system in Belgium and the Netherlands.

I was worried for the sake of those agents still behind the German lines. If this traitor knew so much, then perhaps his masters knew more. I kept my voice level and asked in as casual a tone as I could muster, "Who told you all this?"

He was alert; hope was beginning to trickle back into his veins. "Colonel Kiesewetter of the Abwehr told me. In the Abwehr Headquarters at Driebergen. But who told Colonel Kiesewetter is my secret. Do you wish to make a bargain, sir?"

I was tired and for the moment sick to death of the human degradation confronting me. I had seen many men fight for their lives like cornered rats, prepared to sacrifice employers, country or friends to save their own skins, but somehow I could not stomach this last case of sordid bar-

180

gaining. Having no assistants and no transport, I had to march Verloop back in person to the military prison at the other end of the town. The night was dark and I did not want him to make a break for his life on the journey. So I drew my pistol and looking at him balefully, said, "Come along, Verloop. I have had enough of your scheming. You are a traitor and you are not going to add to your treachery by bargaining with me. Your Nazi friends made the rules for this game. I didn't. So let us play the game their way. Who told those facts to Colonel Kiesewetter?"

The hopeful smile faded. "In exchange for my life, sir . . ." He made a despairing gesture.

I jerked the pistol forward. "Get up." A night of wakeful thought in jail would soon bring him to his senses.

But Verloop, that astute spy, misread my gesture. He thought I was about to shoot him. "Wait," he gasped, "I'll tell you. Don't shoot! It was Chris Lindemans—King Kong. He told Colonel Kiesewetter."

7

So here unexpectedly was the last link that made my chain of evidence against Lindemans complete. I leaned forward and prodded Verloop with the muzzle of my pistol. He went white with fear and gulped. "Did King Kong betray Arnhem to the Nazis?" I asked.

Verloop nodded. He could not speak until he had slipped his tongue over his dry lips and then the words came tumbling from him. "Yes, he told Colonel Kiesewetter on

181

September 15 when he called at Abwehr Headquarters. He said that British and American troops were to be dropped."

"Did he say where?"

"*Ja.* He said that a British Airborne Division was waiting to be dropped on Sunday morning beyond Eindhoven."

I lowered my pistol hand and looked thoughtfully at Verloop. It seemed certain that this miserable coward had pushed the last piece of my jigsaw puzzle into place. He misunderstood the pause and falling on his knees said, "You won't shoot me now, will you? I've told you what I know."

"I won't shoot you myself," I said, "but I can't speak for the Army. A court-martial will decide your fate. Now stand up and let's go."

My years of training in counterespionage work had taught me that giving vent to personal emotions could be a dangerous luxury. But for once I could not control myself. I trembled with a white-hot anger that left me speechless for the moment. Notwithstanding my warning, King Kong had been allowed to go on a secret mission behind the enemy lines where he could do most damage to the Allied cause. Before I had only suspected the truth. Now I knew it, thanks to the shameless traitor Verloop. Nothing could undo the tragedy of Arnhem but at least a summary end could be put to Lindemans' treachery.

Once Verloop was safely in his prison cell, I rushed, still seething with rage, to Dutch Intelligence Headquarters. I burst into the officers' mess. The sight of my fellow countrymen, lolling in their soft armchairs with drinks in their hands, listening to some hurdy-gurdy tune on the radio, made my anger leap to its full tension. I stood there, speechless with fury.

One of my acquaintances looked round. "What's up, Pinto?" he asked. "You look as white as a sheet."

That mild inquiry did it. My anger boiled over. "Turn that damned thing off!" I shouted. I crashed my fist on a table and, as the radio crackled into silence, they all looked at me in surprise. For a second I hated those open-mouthed moon faces turned to mine in astonishment.

"God damn it!" I shouted. "It's high time you lot realized that when I say a man is suspect, I mean it. And what do you do? Straightaway you send him behind the enemy lines with the most vital message of the war!"

"What do you mean?" someone blurted out.

"Lindemans—King Kong. Two of you will go by car to Castle Wittouck at once and arrest him."

"Arrest Lindemans—you must be crazy! Why, with his bare hands he could smash a couple of men like rag dolls. Besides, he's always armed to the teeth. It would be sheer suicide."

One of the senior officers spoke. "In any case, Pinto, what are your grounds for arresting Lindemans? Do you realize the public scandal there would be?"

Rapidly I gave my reasons. Something in my manner must have shown them my sincerity. But there still remained the problem of carrying out the arrest without risking the lives of the escort. And then, as sometimes happens when one is keyed up with excitement, the answer came to me in a flash.

"I have it," I cried. "Two of you—you and you—will go to Castle Wittouck and interview Lindemans. Tell him he is to be decorated for his gallant services. That should appeal to his colossal ego. Persuade him to disarm, put on a clean shirt and brush his hair. Then take him into a private room. In the meantime I will have sent a message by teleprinter to S.H.A.E.F. asking for ten military policemen to be sent to the Castle. When Lindemans enters the room they will overpower him and arrest him. Understood?"

The two officers I had selected grinned and got to their feet. "Fair enough," one said as he buckled on his pistol belt. "I hope ten will be enough for him. Tell S.H.A.E.F. to pick the biggest they've got."

That was the plan—and it worked. As I had suspected, King Kong's vanity was easily assailed. As soon as he heard that he was to be "decorated," lamblike he allowed himself to be shorn of his weapons and, having smartened himself up, was shepherded to the private room set aside for the purpose. Then, swaggering into the private room ahead of his "guard of honor," King Kong advanced to receive his award. It arrived in the shape of the ten military policemen who overwhelmed him and, after a struggle, secured him. There were no handcuffs in Holland big enough to clamp round his mighty wrists so instead his arms were lashed with steel-cored rope. When he was brought onto the R.A.F. airfield at Antwerp I ordered his legs to be bound as well. It was just possible that with the brute strength in

184

his legs he could smash a hole through the thin walls of the aircraft and to plunge to his death from mid-air might be a spectacular last gesture that would appeal to the vanity of King Kong.

When the aircraft touched down in England, Lindemans was rushed to a private country house outside London. It was staffed by the British Counter-Intelligence whose interrogators were possibly the most skilled in the world at extracting a full confession without resorting to any form of physical torture. They were expert at assessing the psychological strength and weakness of their suspects and at breaking down the mental obstacles that held back the truth. For two weeks they kept Lindemans under cross-examination. When he was flown back to Holland, this time pinioned with a pair of Scotland Yard's special adjustable ratchet handcuffs, and lodged in Breda Prison, I escorted him to his cell. I looked at him carefully. Gone was the swagger and the truculence, but there was not a bruise or a wound on his massive body, no puncture marks where a hypodermic needle had been plunged in. His eyes were lowered but there were no telltale signs around them to show that he had been violently frightened or kept awake for days on end. But with him came a full and detailed confession covering twenty-four pages of closely typed foolscap. Without resorting to any kind of torture the experts had sucked King Kong's mind dry of all the self-incriminating facts it contained.

I took the Top Secret confession to my office and sat down to study it. It was more exciting than any detective story and it was satisfying to read the confirmation of much guesswork and deduction. The story of Lindemans' treachery began in 1943 when he was at the height of his fame as a resistance leader of the Dutch Interior Forces. He had always been promiscuous in his sexual tastes and with it vastly extravagant. Running short of funds for lavishing presents on his numerous girl friends, he hit on an ingenious method for supplying his private exchequer. He persuaded rich women, some of them physically attracted by him, to part with their best jewels to provide fighting funds for the "underground" escape route through Belgium and Holland into Occupied France and thence into Portugal. Many of these women whose friends and relatives were only too often languishing in Nazi concentration camps and whose fine houses were billeting German officers were eager to oblige the romantic resistance hero.

Lindemans had sold many of the jewels thus collected but the proceeds never augmented the resistance funds. They were spent in taverns and night clubs in drunken orgies and in buying the favors of girls whose virtue needed dazzling with gold before they would agree to endure the bearlike caresses of the great man. Those jewels which he did not sell he gave away to his mistresses, boasting that they were part of the loot he had taken from the Nazis by force.

Thus far Lindemans had descended to embezzling but he was still an honest man where his country was concerned. Yet although he may not have realized it he was driving down a one-way route. Sooner or later he would

186

have to account for the jewels he had embezzled, unless he could make sufficient money by other means to pay their value into resistance funds. Already one or two of the other resistance leaders were growing suspicious of his extravagant way of living. It was not an easy matter in Occupied Europe to acquire large sums of money suddenly by any honest means and Lindemans began to wonder how he could set about making good his fraud without giving up the extravagance he loved.

Then in February, 1944, an event occurred which must have precipitated the crisis. His youngest brother and the French cabaret dancer named Veronica were captured by the Gestapo in a raid on a house which was a hostel on the secret escape route. In Lindemans' amorous career which featured hundreds of girls, sometimes as many as three or four during the one orgy, Veronica had been the only constant factor. However often he strayed, he always returned to her in the end. If there were room in Lindemans' massive frame for love of anyone but himself, then Veronica occupied that place.

One of the worst moments in any man's life is to know that his dearest friends are in the hands of torturers like the Nazis and, worse, that he can do nothing to rescue them. But it happened every day to one resistance man or the other. All they could do was to clench their teeth and go about their job of revenge with a savage coolness. The good resistance man could not indulge his feelings by a reckless and desperate gesture which might risk the lives of even more of his friends and relatives.

187

But after ten days Lindemans proved to be weaker in moral caliber than his lesser known colleagues. Frantic with worry over the fate of Veronica and his brother and sensing the growing suspicions of other resistance leaders who were beginning to wonder aloud about the fate of the jewels and money entrusted to him, Lindemans decided to make a deal with the enemy. He knew two Dutchmen living in Brussels who were in the pay of the Nazis. One was Anthony Damen, the other Cornelis Verloop, my "friend"of Eindhoven. He arranged to meet them privately in the café of the Hotel des Grands Boulevards on the Place Rogier in Brussels. There over a cup of coffee Lindemans offered his services to the Nazis on two conditions: one, the instant release of Veronica and his youngest brother; two, big money payments. Verloop went off at once to discuss the matter with Giskes, then head of the German Abwehr. Giskes must have realized that here was a golden opportunity of exchanging two minnows for a whale. Two days later he met Lindemans secretly in a house in the suburbs of Brussels where they talked together for a long time.

The bargain was sealed and next day the Germans kept their end of it. Veronica and the youngest Lindemans were pulled out of their dark, damp cells, made to sign certificates to the effect that they had been well treated and were then thrust to freedom in the spring sunlight of the Rotterdam streets. Their joy at the unexpected release could not have been marred by any foreknowledge that this was the first step in a series of events which culminated

188

a few months afterward in the deaths through disease and famine of twenty-five thousand citizens of Rotterdam in the terrible "Black Winter" of Holland.

King Kong, having taken the decisive step into infamy, reveled for a time in the immediate results. He spent the first installments of his traitor's pay in a new burst of revelry, drinking, wenching and fighting tavern brawls with more zest than ever before.

But, as I had suspected during my earlier investigations into his career, his employers, the Abwehr (the German Intelligence) either through a sense of rivalry or because they dared not spread the news too wide had failed to inform the other security branches, the Gestapo and the Security Police, that Lindemans was now in their pay. One day the Security Police raided another Rotterdam resistance headquarters. They burst into the cellar with guns leveled. Lindemans was among the resistance men there!

It was a bad moment for him. He could either give himself away as a traitor in the full view of his Dutch comrades or else risk sudden death at the hands of the S.D. Police. He hesitated for a second and then took the coward's choice. He moved one hand in a certain secret gesture to let the S.D. men know that he was on their side. But before their commander could rasp out the order for his men to avert their rifles, one of them misinterpreted the gesture. Already "trigger-happy" at the great bulk and fierce appearance of King Kong, he thought that the big man was reaching for a revolver. He fired and the bullet hit King Kong in the chest, piercing one lung.

189

He was rushed off to a Gestapo hospital for the S.D. commander realized that here was no ordinary resistance man. The wound would have proved fatal to many humans of average physique but the jungle strength of King Kong brought him through the crisis into convalescence within three weeks. The head of the Abwehr visited him in hospital to make plans for him to "escape" and return to his own side where he could continue to be a valuable agent of the Abwehr. The idea was to arrange a plausible "escape" but Lindemans himself had an ingeniously savage suggestion which made even the hard-headed Colonel gape. It was Lindemans himself who suggested that his own resistance men should attempt the rescue, so that they would walk into an ambush and be killed while he got away. The plan was put into effect and unluckily worked only too well. Forty-seven of his gallant colleagues gave up their lives to rescue their treacherous leader.

For the next few months Lindemans earned his German pay by betraying several groups of agents. One such British group which included women as well as men had been working in the part of Belgium still occupied by the Germans. They were arrested, flung into Scheveningen Prison and there suffered exquisite agony until death mercifully ended their torture. Scheveningen Prison near The Hague contained weirdly ingenious instruments of torture of modern design, beside which the medieval thumbscrew and rack seemed like playthings. There were, for example, steel helmets which were screwed down over the victim's head and eyeballs and then electrified, so that the shock would pierce most keenly to the very nerve centers of the head. When the Germans evacuated the prison they were in too much of a hurry to remove these damning signs of their vicious ingenuity. When I first saw their instruments of torture, contraptions which any sane man could hardly imagine, let alone manufacture and use, my blood ran cold at the sight. And yet Lindemans who could not bear to think of his brother and girl friend being in German hands, cheerfully betrayed whole groups of agents for cash. When I read the list of names, many of whom were known to me and some indeed being my good friends, I vowed that I should not rest until Lindemans had met his deserts.

The climax of his confession was of course the betrayal of Arnhem. When he was attached to the Canadian First Army and given the job of alerting the resistance movement in the Eindhoven area so that they could aid the forthcoming airborne landings, he realized at once that this was a golden opportunity for bigger and better treachery. He completed his Eindhoven mission—not without difficulty for the local resistance leader was suspicious of him and had him arrested. (In fact, with supreme irony as it turned out, the Canadians had to send an intelligence officer to "bail out" Lindemans and vouch for his integrity before the Eindhoven resistance men would listen to his proposals.) Even this setback did not deter him from his traitorous course. He met Colonel Kiesewetter of the Abwehr at Driebergen on the fifteenth of September, two

191

days before the landings were to take place, and told him all the secret facts with which he had been entrusted. It is true that Lindemans did not mention the word "Arnhem." A certain section of the Dutch press subsequently tried to make much of this and claimed that Lindemans could not have betrayed Arnhem because he did not know the exact area of the landings.

This argument is puerile nonsense. Lindemans may not have mentioned the actual name of Arnhem but he did tell Colonel Kiesewetter that the landings were to take place north of Eindhoven. He said as much in his signed confession. Now every large-scale parachute landing, as any amateur tactician should know, is made with the object of seizing some vital area and holding it for a limited length of time. Paratroops, the elite of the army, are too valuable to be scattered aimlessly over the countryside in penny packets. One glance at the map would suffice to tell the German military experts what points these airborne troops would be concentrated on "north of Eindhoven." There was no valuable objective in the open fields. No! the obvious targets were the bridges at Grave, Nijmegen and Arnhem. If these could be seized and held long enough for the main body to link up with the paratroops, then a dangerous bridgehead aimed at the heart of Germany would be developed.

So Lindemans' infamy can never be whitewashed. When he told Colonel Kiesewetter of the Top Secret plan to land airborne forces "north of Eindhoven" in two days' time, he betrayed the Battle of Arnhem.

192

8

It was one thing to vow that Lindemans must be brought to justice and another thing to accomplish that vow. Certain highly placed officials in the Netherlands Forces were, perhaps understandably, reluctant to see Lindemans publicly tried. Some of them who had previously and innocently shown him friendship and favors did not want their lack of judgment exposed to the public eye. Others felt, quite sincerely, that it would not be good for the Dutch war effort if a man who had been a popular and revered figure were to be shown up as an infamous traitor. It was indeed a delicate political and diplomatic situation. So it was that, although I was summoned to S.H.A.E.F. and there congratulated by General Eisenhower himself on the importance of my catch, I was no nearer seeing Lindemans in the dock.

Then came Christmas, 1944, when I fell ill and had to return to London for three months' sick leave. During this time the British newspapers scented out a story of a secret prisoner. Although Lindemans was then still in my private wing at Breda Prison, some news of his being sent to England for questioning must have leaked out. Rumor had it that a Dutch officer was being held prisoner secretly in the Tower of London. This romantic story, or rather, theory, occupied many headlines in the news-hungry press. At my suggestion representatives of the Dutch Government in London approached the British Censorship Department with the request that as the Lindemans Case was still *sub judice,* any public speculation over the reasons for his

193

arrest should be considered illegal. The chief censor agreed and asked the newspapers to drop the subject, which with their customary good sense and public spirit they did.

It was unlikely that anyone would think of bringing Lindemans to justice in my absence and although I chafed at the thought of his continuing to evade his deserts, I was glad to know that he could render no more harm to the Allied cause. In June, 1945, I was able to return to his case and the first thing I did was to order his removal from Breda Prison to that grim block of dungeons nicknamed "The Orange Hotel," which formed part of Scheveningen Prison. There in a cell which had probably been occupied by some of the friends he had callously betrayed, Lindemans would know that he was one step nearer justice.

The solitude, the enforced abstinence for one who had been famed for his sexual prowess, and the further deprivation of that hero worship on which his immense vanity had always battened wrought swift changes in him. His appetite disappeared and the flesh seemed to melt from his bones. Without exercise his huge knots of muscles grew slack and stringy. The giant frame could never be altered but now it grew so gaunt that the clothes hung limply on it as on a scarecrow. His hair went gray and his eyes were dull in their dark sockets. Whenever I visited him he would have a fit and lie frothing at the nose and mouth or grovel on the floor of his cell, shrieking for mercy. What mercy could a man expect, who had betrayed his own friends for cash, who had cost us seven thousand casualties at Arnhem and had prolonged a war for perhaps six months more than

194

was necessary? I could feel nothing but contempt for a man who could not stand the treatment he had cheerfully ordered for others and who had not, like them, felt the keen agony of ingenious torture. I was all the more determined to see him facing his trial.

And so I went back to my office, which was now with the Dutch Counter-Intelligence. I wanted to get hold of the documents in his case and submit them with an urgent request that his trial should take place. The records room at Intelligence Headquarters was closely guarded. Only senior officers on important business were allowed access to the room. Any papers or documents removed had to be scrupulously signed for. Even signatures on papers and identity cards were compared to avoid any possible forgery. A security cordon surrounded the whole building. I had seen many security arrangements in the past and I was certain that few would have equaled the setup there.

But when I went to get the vital file it was not in its proper place. I searched carefully on neighboring shelves and in nearby filing cabinets in case it had been accidentally filed away in the wrong place. There was no sign of it. I checked the record index to make sure that the system had not been reorganized in my absence. There was no entry to show that there ever had been a file on the Lindemans Case. In fact the very name "Lindemans" had been carefully and completely expunged!

I began to make pressing inquiries. At last I learned that a certain senior officer had called for the file some days earlier. I tackled him. He admitted that he had had the file

195

in his possession for a short time but had passed it on to another senior officer. I went to see the latter. When I questioned him he looked blank. No, he had never set eyes on the Lindemans file. I returned to the former senior officer. He was equally surprised. He could have sworn that the other senior officer had taken the file from him on such and such a day. And there the matter ended. From that day to this I have never set eyes on the Lindemans file and there was nothing further for the moment that I could do.

9

In October, 1945, after I had made a nuisance of myself by continually importuning my seniors to bring on the trial of Lindemans, I was suddenly released from the Security Service and later promoted and transferred to duty in Germany. I had, however, been expecting such a move and had in fact joked with my friends about it in advance. There is an old Dutch proverb which says: "He who wants to beat a dog can always find a stick for the job." I had long realized that after the arrest of King Kong a stick would later be found for me.

But I was not sorry for what I had done, only that I had not achieved better results. Love of Holland, my native country, has always taken first place with me, but moreover I have always believed that the people of a country should be big enough to know the truth even if it is not always to their advantage. Most Dutch people did not yet know why Arnhem had failed. They had been taught to

196

blame the weather or "the luck of the game" or Field Marshal Montgomery's recklessness in mounting a daring operation without sufficient resources at his disposal. They did not know that one of their own countrymen had betrayed the battle before it started. It seemed that as long as Lindemans could be kept obscurely in jail—and there appeared to be no time limit to this—they never would know.

And so the months went by and the mud was allowed to settle at the bottom so that on the surface everything was limpid and clear. But in May, 1946, when I had long resigned myself to having heard the last of Lindemans, a surprising event occurred. The British press was of course no longer gagged by censorship. The European war had been over for a full year. The press which has so often championed the cause of the individual against the bureaucracy and has brought sufficient pressure to bear through publicity to put an end to injustice, began to print articles demanding to know what had happened to "the Dutch officer who had betrayed Arnhem," "the secret prisoner in the Tower of London." For several days the press campaign went on; newspapers in England and the Continent of different political outlooks were at one in their desire to know the facts. The same questions were asked by all. The "Dutch officer" had been arrested more than eighteen months before. Had he been tried and, if so, what was the result of his trial? If he had not yet been tried, what was the reason for the delay? In the face of these demands the Dutch Government had only one course to take. It was

197

announced that a Special Tribunal would assemble at the end of June, 1946, for the purpose of trying Christian Lindemans on charges of treason.

(At this stage I must point out that my knowledge of the rest of Lindemans' brief career is based on hearsay and the official Dutch version of his fate. I was no longer in Holland and thus without access to the facts at first sight. If one of the hallmarks of truth is that it really is stranger than fiction, then without doubt the official version is completely true. As it is impossible now to obtain the evidence that would confirm or refute the communiqué, one's only choice is to accept it. Nevertheless, as with all famous mysteries there are loose ends and hidden interrogation marks which cannot be satisfactorily explained—at least to one who likes his evidence cut and dried.)

As I have already mentioned, Scheveningen Prison, perhaps the largest in Holland, had been used by the Nazis for holding political prisoners. Many of Holland's most gallant patriots had been tortured and allowed to rot there. When the Nazis were driven out and the prison was taken over by the Allies, it was found that most of the surviving Dutch prisoners were too ill to be moved. A specially equipped hospital was set up for their treatment inside the main structure of the building and gradually the prison became more and more of a hospital. In fact only one large wing was still used for its original purpose. There the suspected traitors, the collaborators, spies and looters were held, among them Christian Lindemans.

For months Lindemans had been growing weaker. He

198

was now so emaciated that the skin seemed to hang in folds on his giant skeleton. In addition he was partly paralyzed. The Dutch prison doctors, knowing that he had been shot through the lung, suspected that tuberculosis had set in and removed him from his bleak stone cell to the prison hospital for special tests and treatment.

Women nurses are not usually found in Dutch prison hospitals but as Scheveningen was now more of a hospital than a prison the rule was waived in its case. Although Lindemans was no longer the superb muscular athlete with a reputation for turning girls' heads, he must still have possessed some potent spark of manhood, if we are to believe the official version of what happened next. For one of these coldly efficient and practical nurses fell in love with him.

Perhaps they had known each other in the lustier days when Lindemans could pick up a grown man in each huge fist and knock them out by crashing their heads together, could drink enough wine to finish off three ordinary men and could then satisfy three or four girls in the one night with his sexual prowess. Perhaps she had been won by his great reputation as a resistance leader and refused to believe that he was guilty of the charges against him. Whatever the cause, and we shall never know the real motives, she decided to help him to escape the consequences of his approaching trial.

Lindemans was kept in a prison hospital room by himself. The door was locked on the outside; there was only one small window and that was heavily barred. The room

199

was several stories up with a sheer drop of many feet to the ground. It was not a promising situation for any man to escape from, let alone one who was partly paralyzed and in such a physical decline that he was under observation for tuberculosis. But according to the official version, the daring plan nearly worked. The nurse managed to smuggle a steel file into Lindemans' room. With this she had to saw through the stout bars of his window in such a way that although they appeared to be intact, one hard push would remove them. She had an accomplice who had the romantic nickname of "The Singing Rat." He was apparently serving a term of imprisonment for some minor offense; through her efforts, he was given the job of nursing orderly for sick prisoners.

If you have ever tried sawing through strong bars with a file you will know that it is not an easy job, particularly if you have to do it as quietly as possible. Hospital nurses are given many tasks to perform and they never seem to have a spare or an unsupervised moment. Yet here was one who had so much time to spare that she could spend hours in Lindemans' room sawing away at the bars of his cell window without apparently causing any suspicions among her observant colleagues. Certainly she must have taken turns with The Singing Rat at the sawing but even then she must have kept *cavé* near the room in case someone walked in unexpectedly. So much activity in the one place and no one sufficiently observant to comment on it. For any hospital this would be amazing; for a prison hospital it is almost incredible.

200

The second part of the plan was even more difficult to perform. Having prepared the bars so that they could be removed without effort, the three plotters had to devise some means for Lindemans to reach the ground after climbing through the window. His cell was many feet off the ground. There were no convenient footholds or drainpipes down which he could climb. So it was arranged that on the night set for the escape The Singing Rat would leave a rubber hose pipe hanging out of a store-room window which happened to be conveniently close to the window of Lindemans' cell. All the escaper had to do was perch on the window sill of his own room, swing across until he grasped the hose pipe and then swarm down it.

For the man he had been at the time of his arrest this scheme would have presented few problems. His brute strength would have allowed him to climb down almost any length of piping as long as it would support his massive weight. But the Lindemans who now had to make the attempt was an emaciated weakling who was also semi-paralyzed. True, his weight was far less and would put less strain on his arms but this still doesn't make the story a likely one. The Lindemans I had last seen only a few months before was hardly strong enough to tie a knot in a length of stout rope. And yet, presumably still further weakened by continued illness and loss of appetite, he was to attempt a feat in the darkness over which a trained and resolute cat burglar might well have hesitated.

Stranger still, according to the official version, he succeeded in his hazardous attempt. He managed to slither

201

down the hose pipe and reach the ground. Unfortunately he made too much noise in the descent, was heard by the guards patrolling the grounds of the prison and was captured by them. Within a few minutes he was behind bars again.

Now when an important prisoner nearly effects a daring escape a few days before he is to be tried, an escape which must have been engineered with inside help, the authorities usually concentrate their energies on arresting his helpers. It would not have required much imagination or powers of deduction to suspect that the nurse who had devoted so much time to the assiduous care of the prisoner might be implicated in his escape plan. Even if it were impossible to prove her complicity, the safest course would be to allot her duties to some other nurse. But for some unaccountable reason she was neither arrested for her part in the plot nor even removed from her post.

The day of justice was approaching. Soon the whole world would know of Lindemans' guilt and a popular false idol would be smashed forever. But Fate—or human intervention—had one more trick to play on the prosecution. Two days before the trial when the routine inspection of all cells took place, Lindemans was found lying on his bed. He was dead. Across his body lay the nurse, inert but still breathing. Strong emetics were immediately forced down her throat and all the modern aids of medicine were used to bring her round. She recovered and confessed that she had administered eighty aspirin tablets to Lindemans and had herself swallowed an equal number. They had agreed on a suicide pact, she said.

Thus a traitor cheated justice. He was now beyond the reach of the law but what of the person who assisted him in his final escape—the nurse? She was surely liable to face charges, the least of which was grave enough, that of being accessory to the attempted escape of a prisoner, and the worst of which, for the survivor of a suicide pact, was murder. Yet this nurse, whom one would consider lucky to get off with a heavy prison sentence, was never tried in public and subsequently has held responsible official positions in Holland. It is a strange thing which I for one do not begin to understand.

And Cornelis Verloop, that self-admitted traitor, whose evidence first confirmed my suspicions of Lindemans' guilt? He also avoided the embarrassment of facing a public trial and must in fact have been completely exonerated since as far as I know there is no record of his being tried. I have heard from various quarters that he subsequently held an official post in Germany under the Dutch Government. It seems a strange reward for a man who betrayed his country to the enemy and I can hardly believe it.

The Special Tribunal that was to have assembled to try Lindemans was dissolved before it ever met. There were brief reports of his death in a few Dutch papers. The case was officially closed.

And so Lindemans, master traitor, lecherous, vain, brutal and cowardly, found in the end that his luck with women held, although women had contributed so much to his final

203

arrest. If he had not entered the Antwerp Security Camp for the purpose of picking up a couple of girls, I might never have suspected him in the first place.

He was undeniably a traitor. I have met many of them and he was by far the worst, not only in his methods but in the damage he caused. Even if one is not prepared to admit that his actions prolonged the war by more than six months, one must credit—or rather discredit—him with the seven thousand casualties suffered by the gallant "Red Devils of Arnhem," with the deaths in action of his brave resistance men and the slow deaths by torture of the secret agents he betrayed. Because the world has never learned his full infamy through his death before trial, there have been many attempts, some of them officially sponsored, to whitewash his memory. I myself was told by a representative of the Dutch Government in London, when the British press was out to print the facts of his career and his death, to deny that King Kong betrayed Arnhem. But to me he was not a big, irresponsible boy who just blundered into the wrong. He was a sordid traitor who coolly sold his secret information to gratify his gross appetites. For the first time I have written here the full facts as I know them; and where I have had to rely on official "handouts" in the last phase of my story, I have exercised the right to comment on them. It is up to the reader to weigh the evidence before him and to reach his own conclusions.

204

CHAPTER XI

A Forward Glance

IF THE study of history has any practical value, it should surely provide lessons that apply to the present and the future. Man learns largely by experience and history is a recorded form of the many experiences of many people over a long time. I do not claim that the cases I have related in this book are historical facts of international importance, although the Lindemans Case at least had results of more than local interest. But they seem to me to provide a moral which has direct application to the times in which we live.

Let us look on the black side for a moment. As long as there is a Communist regime in Russia, we cannot expect to enjoy peace and full prosperity. The Communist ideology implies a state of world domination and the Politburo presumably never relaxes its efforts in that direction. World domination can be achieved in three ways. One is by supposedly democratic means through which weak but well-meaning Governments form a political alliance with their local Communist party which gradually assumes greater power until it is ready to engineer a *coup d'état*. Czechoslovakia was the classic example of this. Another is by keeping the free nations in such a state of suspense that they

205

overstrain their economies by supplying both "guns and butter," by trying to rearm fully and maintain a high standard of living at the same time. According to the Communist theory capitalist economies with their alternating slumps and booms cannot indefinitely sustain the double burden of rearmament and a high standard of living. Sooner or later the economic system will crash and the ensuing hardships for the masses will, with careful guidance from local Communist cells, result in revolution followed by a Communist Government. This is the "cold war" technique which we have seen in operation for the past few years. The third alternative is domination through a shooting war. Even if they did not gain a decisive victory in arms, the Politburo must know that war on the scale which we have recently experienced creates such havoc, such destruction of property and so many postwar problems of resettlement that its aftermath is a fruitful breeding ground for communism. To the homeless and the despairing any drastic political change may be for the better and cannot in any case be for the worse.

It seems to me, therefore, and the thought has no doubt occurred to many people, that the best we can look forward to for many years is a continuation of the present cold war and the worst we can look forward to is an outbreak of actual war. Just as an athlete does not train for the marathon race by practicing hundred-yard sprints, so, I feel, should we get into mental training by refusing to believe that real peace is just around the corner. Unless a miracle occurs, the present situation with its vague threats and its engineered local battles on the perimeter of the Iron Curtain which are obviously intended to dissipate and drain away United Nations resources may exist for many years to come.

Now there seems to me to be two ways in which we should equip ourselves mentally for the long siege. One is positive, the other negative. Communism may be a perversion of all that is decent and worth living for but nevertheless it gives its disciples a creed, an inspiration. For example, one sees every day the young men and women standing at street corners in all weathers selling the *Daily Worker*. They may be misguided or led by false motives but they are outward symbols of an inner faith, however wicked it may be. They and their Communist counterparts in the trade unions are in a way crusaders, ready to advance their cause by argument and example. It is always easier to propound a hypothesis than to defend a fact but are we really positive enough in our defense of the democratic way of life? Do we merely accept our implicit standards passively or are we prepared to act and argue our case against the Communists?

The negative way of defending ourselves during the cold war period is to improve our Counter-Intelligence system. In so-called peacetime Counter-Intelligence is never praised for its successful prevention of spying because the public never gets to hear of such secret happenings. As with angling it is "the one that gets away" that attracts all the attention. But how many and how big have been the ones that got away! Since 1945, to name only the major agents who were either trapped after they had successfully passed information to the Russians or who have apparently got away with impunity, there have been Alan Nunn May, Alger Hiss, Professor Fuchs, and Professor Pontecorvo. Two Foreign Office officials, Burgess and McLean, have also disappeared mysteriously and, at the time of writing, without trace. We are told the latter two had no access to particularly secret information but the four others were in their own realms the possessors of perhaps the most important secret facts in the world today. If the Russians are now stock-piling atom bombs for eventual use against the free world, then the three scientists mentioned must largely share the blame.

In times of war we expect to sacrifice certain of the rights and liberties of the individual. We undergo censorship, the direction of labor and many regulations which we dislike but realize are essential to the successful prosecution of the war. In times of peace we expect these restrictions on our private liberty to be removed. We are right to have such expectations; it would be ironic if, to defend our democratic way of life, we had to sacrifice all its privileges.

But I do believe that in a time of cold war, our atomic scientists, our diplomats and our political representatives are just as much training and fighting for our cause as are the armed services. When a man volunteers for or is conscripted into the army, he expects to lose certain civilian privileges. He has to obey orders, go wherever in the world he is sent and cannot indulge in the luxury of civilian strikes which the army knows as "mutinies." In the same way a scientist or a diplomat or a politician employed by the Government should be under strict orders and should lose those civilian privileges which are incompatible with security. They have one advantage over the conscript. No one forces them to take up employment under the Government. But once they have done so, they should come under the strict discipline and security regulations that are typical of the armed services.

The task of Counter-Intelligence in peace or war is similar to that of the police. It is, first of all, to prevent spying and acts of treachery against the well-being of the State and, secondly, if such acts are committed, to trace and arrest the person responsible. As I have already pointed out, the successful Counter-Intelligence agent requires certain inborn and fairly uncommon qualities, followed by years of experience and training. On the whole his is a thankless job. He may have to work long and irregular hours, his home life is almost nonexistent and he may have to travel across Europe at the shortest notice. He may not make many friends and he can never indulge in the luxury of discussing his job or describing actual cases, even to his wife. One would expect that a job of this kind, which demands that its candidates must have legal and psychological training, and the knowledge of several European languages, and which involves them in unusual hardships, would be rewarded by a high salary. But the opposite is true. When I was Chief Examiner at the Royal Victoria Patriotic School at a time when this might be considered a key position in the British Counter-Intelligence system, my salary was no more than a fairly competent female stenographer would get. It was then of course wartime and one is prepared to make sacrifices in time of war. But in peacetime it is different. One cannot blame a man whose qualifications would easily earn him over £1,500 a year in industry for being reluctant to join a Government department at a third of that amount. He is not being unpatriotic in the least, no more than the Members of Parliament who voted themselves an increase of one third in salary shortly after they took office.

The answer is a simple one. There are only two ways of attracting recruits to an unpopular industry. One is by raising wages and the other is by improving conditions. The latter course is automatically ruled out in Counter-Intelligence work by the very nature of the work. But it would not cost many thousands a year, possibly no more than one per cent of the public money lost in the Groundnuts fiasco, to ensure a really efficient Counter-Intelligence organization with a stream of worthwhile volunteers eager and ready to enlist.

Stinting security is almost the worst form of miserliness, because in the end it costs the dearest. If the Russians ever unloose on the free world atom bombs constructed by the knowledge supplied to them by Nunn May or Fuchs, the cost of repairing the damage will be incalculable and no kind of payment will bring back to life those who are killed in the bombing. Yet a few thousand pounds properly spent at the right time might have kept the secret information intact. Let us never forget that a pennyworth of pre-

210

vention is, atomically speaking, worth a million pounds of cure.

Thus far we have discussed what should be done in terms of cold war. We must remember that, at Russia's whim, the war may turn "hot" at any time. In spite of the great efforts being made to equip and consolidate European defenses, many months, even years, may pass before the task is completed. It would hardly be an exaggeration to estimate that if the Russian hordes suddenly attacked westward in the next few months, they would probably reach the Channel coast within a fortnight of the start of hostilities. The flood of refugees into England might then be ten times what it was after Dunkirk. Today there is a far more potent and better organized Fifth Column in the British Communist party than there was in aid of Hitler over a decade ago. The problems of such a war might be similar to those we have already undergone but much intensified.

To cope with its increased task, if it has not already done so the Counter-Intelligence leaders here should train large numbers of investigators without delay. The Field Security Service, a branch of the Army's Intelligence Corps, is probably the best cadre for training both serving soldiers and Territorials as investigators. Particular importance should be given to teaching investigators how to search luggage, for as certain of the cases I have related have shown, a spy is nearly always given away by some item he brings with him. In addition, noncommissioned officers of the Field Security Service should be taught to speak foreign languages fluently, in particular French and German. During

211

the last war many of these intelligent and reasonably educated men were quite useless, in fact a positive hindrance, to the task of investigation because they could neither interrogate suspects nor even translate their documents.

As the Latin tag succinctly puts it—*si pacem vis, para bellum*. None of us wants to see another war which, win or lose, might well be the end of all our civilization. But war will not be avoided by blanching and throwing up one's hands at the mere thought of it. The Politburo alone can decide whether there is to be war or peace. But even the inmates of the Kremlin are unlikely to start a war unless they are reasonably confident of winning it. The greater our resolution and state of preparedness, the less likely is the Politburo to begin open hostilities.

Since 1936 wars have not only been a conflict of nations but also a conflict of ideologies. Even now some brilliantly intellectual but emotionally juvenile scientist in atomic research may be contemplating betraying secrets to the enemy. Even now some sincere but misguided fanatics may—in fact probably are—plotting to create major industrial unrest to further the Communist cause among the workers of the free world. Our rulers should be "infiltrating" their own agents into local Communist cells, should be greatly increasing the salaries of Counter-Intelligence agents, should be tightening up the discipline of Government research units and also of the Foreign Office and should be making all arrangements for the competent interrogation of refugees in the event of an actual war. I sincerely hope that they are.

212

For although Counter-Intelligence agents are humorously referred to as "cloak and dagger" men, never forget that a cloak is a form of protection and a dagger can pin down the King's enemies.